THE
GRAPHENE
MENTALITY
IN THE AGE OF DISTRACTION

THE GRAPHENE MENTALITY

IN THE AGE OF DISTRACTION

BUILD MENTAL STRENGTH TO DREAM, DARE, AND DELIVER

LT COL SANJEEV MALIK

JAICO PUBLISHING HOUSE

Ahmedabad Bangalore Chennai
Delhi Hyderabad Kolkata Mumbai

Published by Jaico Publishing House
A-2 Jash Chambers, 7-A Sir Phirozshah Mehta Road
Fort, Mumbai - 400 001
jaicopub@jaicobooks.com
www.jaicobooks.com

THE GRAPHENE MENTALITY
ISBN 978-81-988454-1-2

First Jaico Impression: 2025

Page design and layout by Jojy Philip, Delhi

Printed by
Nutech Print Services - India, New Delhi

Contents

III. IGNITE AND RECHARGE

IV. POWER AND PROTECT

A Special Request from the Author

My dear reader, I would like to take this opportunity to request that you do something really important. Please get a pencil. It's a priceless treasure (you will gradually understand why I'm calling it that). If you already have a pencil with you, fantastic! If not, please go and get one immediately before you move on to the next task. Yes, it's that essential.

Why? Because this simple act is the most crucial step in extracting the maximum value from this book. Once you have a pencil with you, give it a nice, clean sharpen. When you do this, you'll be able to connect more deeply with this priceless treasure and succeed in harnessing its limitless worth and power.

Now, I strongly recommend that you use this pencil for two specific purposes here.

One, you should underline the content, tactics, strategies, rituals or methodologies that you believe you've neither read before on the internet or in literature, nor ever heard from century-old philosophers, meditative monks or spiritual tutors. It is my honest belief that the concepts and edicts you'll be reading in this book are, directly or indirectly, a progeny of this magical object you're holding. This pencil encapsulates this new concept of The Graphene Mentality, which you will be introduced to as you steadily move ahead through these pages.

Two, if you want to become a practical lion and not just a theoretical tiger of this novel mindset, you must complete the homework at the end of each chapter with the help of this pencil. As you know, theory without practice is a futile exercise, a nightmare, a dreadful experience, whether it is a semester viva, engine repair, tumor excision, building a bridge, or for that matter, even reading a book.

So, I politely request you to be a conscientious student and do your homework sincerely, taking down notes and internalizing all relevant dictums. If you do that, I promise that by the time you finish this book, you'll get a special all-weather template for a successful and enriching life—a profound recipe to accomplish your most coveted goals. And you will realize that the pencil that you've used to write letters, words, sentences, paragraphs, pages, articles, essays and manuscripts (if you are a budding writer or an established author) is more than just a pencil for writing text. It is a rich repository of unique attributes, which you can assimilate and deploy to write your history and legends, worth endorsing in archives for posterity.

Introduction

It was a bright Sunday morning in Bengaluru. I woke up to the roaring sound of bikers racing past my residence, which abutted the National Highway on the outskirts of this sprawling metropolis. Sunday mornings are the only time these rapturous bikers have plenty of space and time to ride their majestic bikes to fetch barrels of euphoria.

As usual, the moment I woke up, I reached for my journal and the graphite pencil kept on my bedside table. This is a morning ritual I've been following ever since I instilled *the habit* of jotting down wonderful thoughts and ideas that spring to my mind when I'm semi-awake and before I get out of bed. But this time, instead of writing in my notebook, I kept staring at my pencil, examining it for hours. Days passed and months elapsed as I tried to decode the worth of this innocuous-looking object that I have been using to scribble bizarre words and figures since I was a toddler.

Meanwhile, the Covid-19 pandemic started wreaking havoc on an unprecedented scale. The entire country was put under lockdown after Prime Minister Narendra Modi announced his abrupt decision through the national media. As a medical professional, I was working ceaselessly to enforce Covid-19 containment measures, yet I felt a sense of emptiness and despair due to the complete lockdown. The National Highway adjacent to my home, which a few months ago had been a bustling, noisy zone, was now desolate and silent. It seemed that all Homo sapiens had vanished and a new species would soon take their place, just as they had replaced the Neanderthals about 60,000 years ago. The situation perfectly resembled the harrowing scene from *Avengers: Endgame*—as if Thanos had incarnated as Covid-19 to unleash hell on Earth.

To combat the melancholy, people started exploring various skills and exhibited their unique talents on social media. This period saw the emergence of a new genre of social media artists —painters, singers, dancers, scholars, chefs and fitness experts—all desperately trying to flush out the cortisol accumulated because of stress due to prolonged confinement at home.

But I remained in my usual contemplative mode, diligently seeking answers to the questions that kept troubling me. These questions that constantly assailed me (*and I presume you too*) were:

What is the purpose of our life?

What are our aspirations?

Why are we living an individualistic and self-centered life? Are we really concerned about organizational goals or the collective welfare of society?

Why do we fervently pursue transient pleasures such as wealth, prestige, power and fame, which hold little inherent value?

What is the primary motivation behind our actions? Are we solely motivated by external factors and lack a strong internal drive? How much weight do these external factors hold when our health is impacted or relationships are strained?

Why are most of us not living a meaningful and productive life? Why do we spend more time on social media and less on work?

There is plenty of empirical research that says that we spend just 2.5 hours a day on productive tasks. Almost 21% of our work hours are spent on entertainment, news and social media. What a phenomenal waste of our precious time and talent! The remaining hours are consumed by routine chores like cooking, cleaning, eating, sleeping, etc. Many of us are accustomed to the pernicious habit of multi-tasking during work hours and due to this, we fail to complete even a single task. At the end of the day, we're left with a huge backlog of work and carry our files and laptops back home, only to ruin our precious family time.

Are we classic epitomes of inefficiency, and self-saboteurs of the highest degree?

Why do we suffer from indecisiveness when we pick up our smartphones to order food from Zomato? Why do we always find ourselves with the dilemma of choosing between Covishield and Covaxin even though we know that both vaccines have equal efficacy?

Why are we so capricious by nature and seasonally change our decisions? With the advent of spring, we pledge to do something remarkable, and by the time autumn arrives, we lose commitment, energy and the drive to persist with what we've begun. Why do we lack firmness and tenacity to follow through?

Why do we get terrified after failures? And abandon our dreams so easily? Why can't we show resilience to fight back? Or display flexibility to review and revamp our strategy?

These questions perturbed me every time my mind drifted into an alpha state (an alpha state of mind is when we're in wakeful rest, not concentrating on any task). Strangely, the answers to all these questions were hidden in the graphite pencil that had captured my investigative mind since that Sunday morning. I knew already that under the veneer of its simple appearance, the pencil possessed a priceless element, graphene. But I never imagined that this element could be the source of such a wonderful concept— The Graphene Mentality. It was this revolutionary mindset I had been searching for through my questions.

Just as the element graphene was discovered unexpectedly, The Graphene Mentality was also a revelation to me. When Professors Andre Geim and Kostya Novoselov first examined flakes from bulk graphite under a microscope in 2004, they were fascinated by what they found. Similarly, I was exhilarated when I unearthed this unique mindset—a mindset with the potential to redefine the very model of success. It was a true Eureka! moment for me, just as it had been for Archimedes.

I.

Decoding the Graphene Mentality

CHAPTER 1

What Is the Graphene Mentality?

The Graphene Mentality entails specific values and attributes that resemble properties of the element graphene.

So, what are these unique properties of the element graphene?

First and foremost, it is the only element in nature that is two hundred times stronger than steel and yet highly flexible and transparent. Second, it is highly resilient and can sustain a tremendous amount of stress and strain without breaking. Third, what renders phenomenal strength to this wonder element is the peculiar structure and arrangement of its atoms. Embodying perfect team spirit, each atom of the element is intimately bound to three other atoms, creating a solid structure responsible for its inherent strength and resilience.

Please have a look at the structure of the element Graphene and you will get a better picture of what I am talking about.

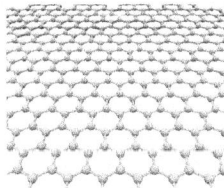

ELEMENT **GRAPHENE**

Because of these properties, it has enormous utility in a wide array of industries—electronics (manufacturing batteries with super-fast charging, bendable smartphones, flexible touch screens), lighter aircrafts, strong and durable helmets, sturdy sports gear (tennis rackets, golf clubs, shoes and clothes). The list is endless. It is counted among the most versatile substances.

These fundamental properties of firmness, flexibility, resilience and team spirit, which this element exhibits, constitute the cardinal values of The Graphene Mentality.

To understand it clearly, look at the image below. Now, visualize atoms of the element graphene becoming strongly embedded in the 86 billion neurons of your mind, blending all their unique properties into your mindset. The essence of The Graphene Mentality lies in its four core atoms—each symbolizing a distinct, life-changing value. This concept moves the utility of graphene beyond the tangible domain of industries and explores its potential and application in the intangible realm of psychology.

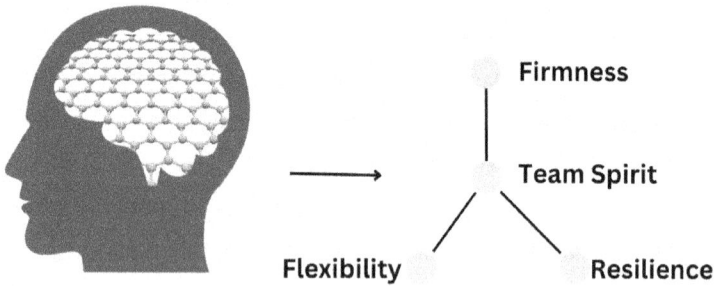

Firmness

Team Spirit

Flexibility

Resilience

CHAPTER 2

Why Do You Need the Graphene Mentality?

For centuries, many noble virtues have been competing to become worthy ingredients for success. Hard work, smart work, sincerity, honesty, courage, discipline, patience and persistence. And there are many more on the list. Some achievers advocate hard work and discipline, some vouch strongly for smart work and courage, and some emphasize honesty and sincerity, depending on what worked for them while they executed their iconic deeds.

In this maze of highly cherished values, we rarely find mention of flexibility, firmness, resilience and team spirit. These values are often neglected by CEOs, personal coaches, academic gurus, motivators and mentors in their mission statements. They are kept on a lower pedestal, maybe because such values appear innocuous to them and don't evoke as much sentiment as values like hard work and courage do. Maybe they believe that values like honesty and dedication are more inspiring to people when compared to flexibility and firmness. Or it could be that they believe that individual perseverance is a more effective and a focused strategy than team effort. This is a huge misconception!

Allow me to propound this central tenet: the values of firmness, flexibility, resilience and team spirit are as essential as other cherished ideals to achieve the critical goals that you've visualized in your dreams. Regardless of the nature of your goals—whether they are related to your career, or associated with your family, or connected to your health—you will definitely need these values to accomplish them. It is immaterial whether you're into business, academics, research, art, theatre or sports. With a mindset that is firm, flexible, resilient and cooperative, you'll always succeed in capturing your targets.

It is often said that there is no one-size-fits-all approach to success. It differs from individual to individual based on inherent qualities and gifts or the different values they like to espouse and nurture. But that does not mean there can't be one practical approach. One approach that is universal in its application, and that requires specific values that are fundamental to success, irrespective of whether you are a hard worker or a smart worker, a disciplined or an erratic person, a fearless or a timid character.

The Graphene Mentality is that practical approach. It provides an ideal template to guide you at every step of your journey to success. This schematic diagram depicts how we can apply

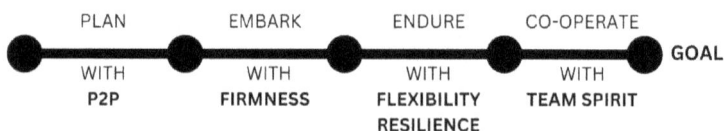

PLAN	EMBARK	ENDURE	CO-OPERATE	
WITH	WITH	WITH	WITH	**GOAL**
P2P	FIRMNESS	FLEXIBILITY RESILIENCE	TEAM SPIRIT	

**ACHIEVING GOALS THROUGH
ATTRIBUTES OF
THE GRAPHENE MENTALITY**

various attributes of The Graphene Mentality at different stages to achieve all of our momentous goals.

Every step in this process is a scrupulous exercise in itself. First, you must do the preparatory homework of P2P and plan what goals to set for yourself. Then, you embark on the journey to your goals with utmost firmness and unwavering focus. Next comes the stage of enduring stress and setbacks (an inevitable part of the goal-chasing process) with attributes of flexibility and resilience.

Finally, remember that winning is not an individual game; it is a team game. It is not a solitary battle; it is a collective war! You need to cooperate with your colleagues selflessly, for it is the most economical and efficient method of winning and an effortless and speedy way to reach your destination.

Now, let's start leveraging The Graphene Mentality.

II.

Leveraging the Graphene Mentality

STEP 1: **PLAN**

'It must be borne in mind that the tragedy of life doesn't lie in not reaching your goal. The tragedy lies in having no goal to reach.'

– Benjamin E. Mays

CHAPTER 3

Choose Your Goals through P2P

What you will learn in this chapter

- How should we choose our goals?
- What is P2P?

Choosing our goals is the first step to success.

But before deciding our goals, let us deconstruct: what is success? We need to know the meaning of success because it is the most misunderstood term of the 21st century. *Merriam-Webster* defines success as "the attainment of wealth and fame."

Is it the correct definition of success?

I don't think so.

Have you not seen the so-called rich and famous people suffering from greed, envy, drug addiction and lust? How can these people be declared successful when they have all these sufferings and perverse instincts pestering them from within?

Then, there is a second definition of success by business gurus, coaching academies, teachers and various rating agencies in the market. They define success as the "accomplishment of outcomes, goals and objectives."

It is common to come across such statements: Amir Khan has delivered five consecutive successful movies, Virat Kohli has completed 10,000 runs in cricket, ABC coaching academy produced a brilliant result this year and 500 candidates succeeded in cracking the IIT/JEE exam, *Forbes* has listed the 100 most successful companies and the top 10 start-up unicorns of this year.

This definition of success, which is based exclusively on metrics and outcomes, also appears to be wrong on account of the following two reasons.

The first is that it is grossly unfair to label a person successful or unsuccessful based on just the outcome or results of their efforts. Any outcome is a product of various closely intertwined factors like aptitude, luck, guidance, mentoring, parental support and opportunity. Then, don't you think that when we label a person as unsuccessful, we should also consider other factors?

It might be that a person didn't have the best luck, or didn't receive adequate guidance, or did not get the ideal opportunity and platform to demonstrate talent. I mean, there could be hundreds of reasons for being unsuccessful. So, this systemic stigmatization of an individual as unsuccessful by myopic naysayers is preposterous. I believe that no one holds the license, authority or experience to predict, or pronounce a verdict on, the life and prospects of anyone on this planet.

Now, coming to the other reason why the second definition of success is wrong.

It is an irrefutable fact that setting goals and objectives makes us more sincere, disciplined and accountable. Plus, the process of goal-setting is a significant motivating factor and constantly centers us when we drift away from our path. However, the tragedy is that most of us set our goals unrealistically, without doing the homework of aligning them with our intrinsic passions. We want to do a thing because we want to do it, and not because we love it. And in a case worse than this, we want to do a thing because our parents, friends or relatives want us to do it. The initial goal-setting is itself wrong.

In this scenario, even if we accomplish our goals, we still feel unhappy and dejected, as our work is not in congruence with our inherent passion. And though we may call ourselves successful, and society also perceives us to be so, we're unsuccessful because we're constantly disenchanted with our work. We keep sulking about our profession in a disgruntled manner, thus ruining our happiness and jeopardizing our career prospects. This is the delusional model we follow while setting goals.

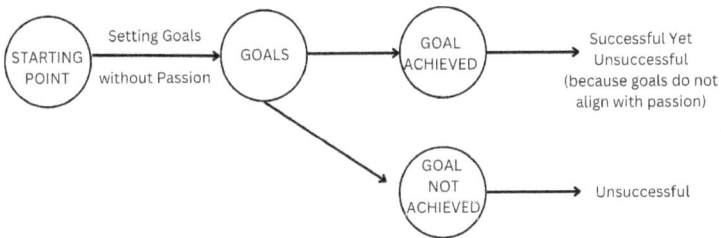

DELUSIONAL MODEL OF GOAL-SETTING

The Realistic Model of Goal-Setting

It is time to discard the existing delusional model and follow a more realistic one, which looks something like the one depicted in this section.

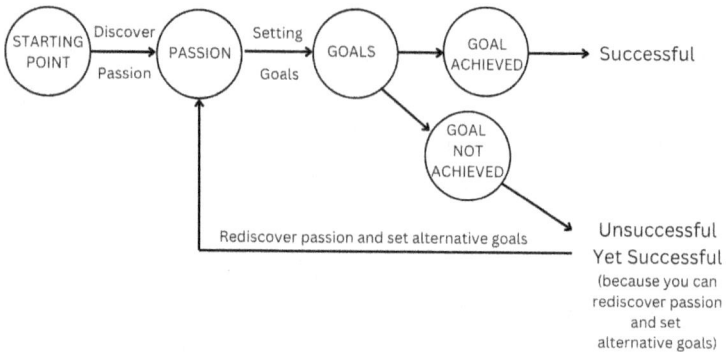

REALISTIC MODEL OF GOAL-SETTING

If you apply this realistic model in your lives, you will live a happier and more meaningful life. Under this model, even if you fail in accomplishing your goals and society deems you to be unsuccessful, you can rediscover your passion, set alternative goals, and live a successful life endowed with inner satisfaction and contentment.

Let me illustrate this model with a real-life example.

Dr Roman Saini is an inspirational figure. Not many people have heard his name but he is an iconoclast with an out-of-the-box mentality. At 21, he cleared the UPSC civil services, among the world's toughest exams, and secured an All-India Rank of 16. He joined the prestigious Indian administrative cadre in 2014. But very soon, he resigned from the service, a decision which shocked his batchmates. They wondered, "Why would anyone risk his career by making such a foolish decision?" Many surmised that he was afraid to take the challenging job of a civil servant or was not ready to assume massive responsibility in this field.

However, he relinquished the job because he discovered that it was not his passion and he realized it would not make him happy. He did not want to be a victim of the delusional model.

With his daredevil instincts, he ventured into a domain perhaps more perilous than the civil services. He set forth his new goal of becoming an entrepreneur! In 2015, along with his friends Gaurav Munjal and Hemesh Singh, he co-founded Unacademy, India's largest online learning platform. Unacademy delivers educational content to millions of students who can't afford to pay exorbitant fees at offline coaching academies. It has disrupted the entire landscape of education. His platform has made education an accessible and affordable resource by connecting students to expert teachers across the length and breadth of the country. Today, his company is valued at $3.4 billion, and with 50,000 educators teaching and mentoring 60 million students, it is one of the fastest growing start-ups in the education sector.

Roman is doing remarkably well as an entrepreneur because his passion for educating people and transforming their lives is steering him forward. And I am sure that one day, he will succeed in his eventual goal of expanding this platform to every nook and corner of the world and bring it to many more students across the globe.

He is a proponent of the realistic model.

Another person who is an embodiment of the same model, and who I know personally, is Major (Dr) Surendra Poonia. He is a fitness expert and quite popular across all social media platforms. We both have the same pedigree. We graduated from the same medical college (he was ten years senior to me), we both are paratroopers and served as doctors in the Special Forces. However, he was not so keen to continue his career in medicine and willingly chose not to do a post-graduation course that 99% of doctors do. His passion was different. He was a naturally gifted athlete and was obsessed with running all the time—be it early morning, afternoon, evening or late at night. Even during working hours when everyone would expect him to be in the office, he would don his Nike vest and shoes and head outdoors for a long run. He set his own fitness goals, broke them into daily targets, and would sweat profusely to finish them before he slept.

His friends, parents, relatives and even senior officers in the regiment condemned him for his decision to not pursue a career in medicine. But he was unfazed by the opinions and attitude of others because he knew that he was running on the right track, as his goals were in absolute harmony with his passion. He never quit running and went on to win 27 medals for his country in three back-to-back World Medicine and Health Games—a sports tournament organized for doctors across the globe. It was a stupendous feat for which he gained a spot in the Limca Book of Records!

The story did not end here. Like Roman, he also became an entrepreneur. In fact, I would call him a fitpreneur. And few years back, in partnership with his colleague Mrs Shilpa Bhagat, he built *Fitistan: Ek Fit Bharat*—a digital platform to cultivate fitness among the masses. It is a community-driven initiative that motivates people to participate in various fitness challenges such as HIIT, calisthenics, walkathons and marathons. The modus operandi of *Fitistan* is to create an army of fitness ambassadors, known as Fit Captains who would take this initiative further and spread the importance of a healthy lifestyle in society. As of now, there are 4.5 lakh members who are actively taking this mission forward.

"My ultimate dream is to make a FIT BHARAT," gushed Major Poonia when I asked him about the purpose behind launching *Fitistan*. "I want to bring people across all age groups and segments on this platform for their health and longevity. My agenda is clear: I want to make fitness an inseparable part of their life. And that's why I keep my fitness challenges as simple as possible, modelled on the four laws of atomic habits: make it obvious, attractive, easy and rewarding," he summed up succinctly.

Though Roman and Major Poonia are doctors through education, they made key adjustments in their career trajectory by pursuing goals attuned to their passion. One is dedicated to offering an all-in-one solution for education needs, while the other is committed to operating a centralized hub for fitness. But their shared trait is the gumption to espouse the realistic model of success.

The realistic model propagates this fundamental principle: when choosing our goals, we should never disregard our priceless autonomy. Do not do what your parents are forcing you to do, what your peers recommend, or what is fashionable and trending in the market.

Here is the rational proposition: identify the unique talent and skill which you are gifted with, and then set your career goals and objectives accordingly. If you like studying the humanities, then it is foolhardy to opt for courses like medicine or engineering. Vice-versa, if you are a genius in mathematics and science, there is no point in doing courses in the humanities.

Also, there is no conventional principle that a career can be built only through relentless studies, knowledge enhancement and academic pursuits. If you are not motivated to study and have an intense phobia of books, there is nothing wrong with it. It is just human physiology and not some weird pathology. Explore the other remarkable gifts that you possess such as sports, singing, dancing or painting. Build your career accordingly. It's always fruitful to carve your own path because when you follow the herd mentality and jump onto the bandwagon of others, you trigger your downfall, setting the stage for your doomsday. You lose your individuality considerably and spoil your inherent strengths.

Therefore, you ought to act wisely before selecting your goals.

But what if you end up choosing the wrong goals that do not align with your intrinsic passion? Don't worry. It's never too late. If something is not working out, it is better to change it. Only your ego compels you to cling to unaccomplished goals, even when your soul is fully conscious that these goals are not meant for you. Your ego signals to your brain that if you discard your original goals, you will face rejection, condemnation and ridicule from society. But remember that it is always beneficial to prioritize nourishing your soul than to keep feeding your ego.

It's time to become flexible and change course by adopting the realistic model. Rediscover your passion and reconfigure your goals accordingly.

Correct Definition of Success

The realistic model yields a correct and complete definition of success for all of us. This definition needs to be taught in schools, management institutes, seminars and webinars, to thousands of next-generation potential achievers.

The definition is: "Success is not merely the accomplishment of goals; it is the accomplishment of goals that we are passionate about and which make us happy."

Success should be evaluated daily, and we must constantly introspect whether we're going down the right path. We must ask ourselves whether we'll discover passion and excitement through the goals we have planned for our lives.

HOW TO DISCOVER PASSION?

While choosing the goals we are passionate about, a tenable question arises: how do we discover our passion?

What do you think is passion? Is it simply doing something we love to do? If you believe that, you might be wrong.

Let me clarify that passion is not just loving something. It is the driving force that propels your actions day and night to pursue that thing, even if you start despising it. The fact is that enthusiasm, intensity and desire start petering down after recurrent failures, setbacks, despair and exhaustion. It is at this point you are truly tested about whether you are passionate about something or not. If you're fond of playing musical instruments, devote your precious hours to percussion and striking your favorite chords, even if you get bored. If you harbor an ambition of winning the Grand Slam, pick up your racket and sweat out with intense gusto, even if you hate doing it.

The willingness to suffer defines passion. According to Kevin Hall, author of *Aspire: Discovering Your Purpose through the Power of Words*, the true meaning of passion is *to suffer*. Passion is the sacred suffering for the activity you love to do and is not simply a source of pleasure.

Hence, you need to discover one thing or activity you would still love to do even if you are inflicted with massive aches and pains while doing it. Or, explore a cause that drives you forward even if you're knocked down and pummeled repeatedly. Find something for which you're willing to sacrifice all your other personal interests. When you find that, you will have found your true passion.

P2P: PURPOSE TO PASSION

The most essential step after identifying what you are passionate about is to determine purpose. Purpose should be positive and meaningful. It could be selfless service, social welfare, self-enrichment, physical and mental well-being or preserving the environment around you. However, if selfishness, envious competitiveness, pretentiousness or any other negative purpose pervades your goals, then instead of burning in the fire of your passion, you'll be incinerating in the inferno of your ego, running the risk of turning your ambitions into ashes.

For example, the reason behind sweating out at 5am should not be to flaunt a lean and muscular body and derive pleasure from the admiration of your peers and colleagues. Instead, the aim of daily physical workouts should be to experience inner satisfaction and contentment, born out of the sudden gush of positive hormones released in situ after the workout session.

Similarly, the motive behind studying any subject, doing research, and earning degree after degree should not be to project to the outside world that you know better than others because you have more titles with your name. The purpose should be to enhance knowledge and benefit society by disseminating what you have assimilated through study.

I want to illustrate the need for harmony between passion and purpose through the following insightful interaction between me and one of my senior officers. After observing the volumes of history books and current affairs magazines by my side, and knowing that I was preparing for civil services, he asked me, "Doctor, why do you want to join the civil services?"

"Sir, I want to serve this society in a significant and productive way. And I think I have the right talent and skills to do that," I replied confidently.

"What more service do you want to do? You are a doctor in the Indian Army and have been serving for the last 12 years. Is not that a significant and productive contribution? What more do you want?" he appended.

"Sir, joining the civil services would broaden my domain and perspective. Besides that, I would have more resources and power to implement changes in society."

"Smart Tiger (though I was not smart at all; in fact, he should have called me seduced or hypnotized tiger), that means you're chasing power and resources more than the service. Your purpose is to attain privileges, fame and a name that comes with being a civil servant in our society." He continued further, "And remember dear, it's not that only civil servants are ordained to serve society and implement changes around us. There are many other unsung heroes who are serving in a more magnificent manner such as doctors, engineers, scientists, NGO workers, firefighting squads, disaster rescue teams and entrepreneurs."

This conversation was an eye opener for me. Whatever we're pursuing, the motivating factors for most of us are essentially the same: power, privileges, wealth and fame. To be sure, some people are truly committed to the service and stick to their ideals despite enormous inducements and allurements *otherwise*. But the majority of us project a façade of service but lack strong inherent motivation. And when the façade is removed, we struggle to generate daily vigor and enthusiasm required to do selfless service.

The bottom line is that when the passion is not backed with purpose, passion loses its drive. Purpose is the fuel for passion.

Also, those who embark on their goal journey without being backed by a positive purpose are more vulnerable to material wants, corruption, lust, hooliganism and other nefarious deeds. Several fabled personalities in the past have fallen prey to such nasty impulses after achieving their impassioned aims, regardless of the segment of society that they belonged to—politics, business, sports or entertainment. Business tycoon Vijay Mallya, cyclist Lance Armstrong, golfer Tiger Woods, heavyweight boxer Mike Tyson, wrestler Sushil Kumar, and film producer Harvey Weinstein are popular names. These achievers were intensely passionate and hungry to accomplish more, but paradoxically, they lacked a strong, honorable purpose. This eventually led them to commit perverse and sinister acts that brought them ignominy, disrespect and even life imprisonment.

So, identify the positive and constructive purpose behind your goals, and abstain from choosing negative ones. This beautiful anecdote from the epic *Mahabharata* depicts how a negative purpose can be hazardous to your ambitions.

At Dronacharya's *gurukul*—a renowned institution in Aryavarta (land of Aryans)—two warrior clans, Kauravas and Pandavas, learnt archery under the supervision of their guru. During one of the teaching sessions, Karna, a student who later became an accomplished archer, suddenly appeared and sought admission to the *gurukul*. When Drona asked about his identity, Karna revealed that he was the son of a charioteer. Drona became agitated and refused to train him, citing the bigoted reason that archery was a special skill meant to be learnt by only the elite castes, *Brahmins* and *Kshatriyas*. When Karna contested his statement and asked him why all segments of society could not attain knowledge, Drona got exasperated. This led to a heated argument between the two and Karna was expelled from the *gurukul* immediately.

Karna's questioning held merit and logic, but his final words before leaving the *gurukul* are worth examining. He boasted that he would surpass all of Drona's disciples to become the greatest archer in the world and one day, with his archery skills, he would annihilate this caste-dominated society. This desire for superiority over everyone eventually proved detrimental for Karna, as was evident on the 17th day of the battle of Kurukshetra in the *Mahabharata*. During a face-off with Arjuna, Karna's chariot got stuck in the mud and he could not summon his divine weapon, the *Vijay Dhanush* or the Victory Bow. At this stage, Lord Krishna appeared and questioned him, "Karna, do you know why knowledge has betrayed you in this moment of crisis? It is because throughout your life, you have tried to be superior to Arjuna, and even when you sought divine archery under Lord Parshuram, your focus was more on defeating him than on obtaining knowledge."

Karna failed because his purpose was vitiated. Though he was a passionate archer and was touted as better than Arjuna, his fate was decided the day he set his purpose to become superior to Arjuna instead of focusing on building excellence in his craft.

If a wicked purpose powers our goals, it can sabotage our prospects for success. Powering our goals with a sacred purpose is the only way to succeed.

Takeaways

- Choose your goals through the realistic model of goal-setting.

- Use P2P (purpose to passion) while choosing your goals.

- Keep your purpose strong and positive if you intend to sustain your passion.

PENCIL WORK

☞ On a big sheet of paper or a chart, document your passion. It could be any of these: reading, writing, teaching, travelling, adventure, fitness, business, social service, etc.

☞ Decide on one or two goals with respect to your passion and construct a realistic model depicting these goals. Most people do this the other way around—they decide their goals first and then search for their passion, which is a sure-shot recipe for failure. Don't plan anything else until you are done with these goals.

STEP 2: **EMBARK**

ATOM 1

FIRMNESS

'Be like the promontory against which the waves continuously break, but it stands firm and tames the fury of the water around it.'

– Marcus Aurelius

CHAPTER 4

Firmness

'The First Atom' of the Graphene Mentality

What you will learn in this chapter

- The role firmness plays during two key stages of your goal journey.
- How 'goal pyramid' and 'goal pillar' are significant in building firmness.
- The 4D elements that can damage your goal pillar.

Once you choose your goals through the realistic model of goal-setting and are sure about your purpose, you can embark with firmness, which is the first atom of The Graphene Mentality. The atom of firmness provides the strong traction that enables you to remain steadfast in the decisions that you have taken concerning your goals and objectives. This atom determines your trajectory—whether you will move straight and fiercely in the direction of your dreams, or whether you will wobble on the track and seek an alternate route for an easy escape. Firmness is especially important in contemporary times when the abundance of choices has led to the grave pathology of a fleeting mindset, which makes us hop seamlessly from one goal to another.

But have you ever wondered why we wander like monkeys from one branch to another when it comes to pursuing our goals?

It is because of the fundamental indecisiveness that we all exhibit with respect to day-to-day decisions in our life. You might ponder: how are these routine decisions related to our goals? But the elementary truth is that this indecisiveness at a micro level is reflected at the macro level, too. It adversely impacts our ability to begin, as well as to remain firm on essential goals in our bucket list.

Decision paralysis is the major impediment to building firmness. We must first clear the cobweb of decision paralysis from our minds before we gather the firmness required for embarking on our goals.

DECISION PARALYSIS – THE MAJOR IMPEDIMENT

It is a ruthless reality that when asked to decide on something, a majority of people respond in the following two autopilot modes: *"We will discuss it later"* and *"I will think about it."* And the worst part is that when they recourse to such automated responses, they're not discussing or thinking about anything else either. Yet they keep procrastinating, and by behaving in these default modes, they fail to initiate vital decisions.

Frankly, I, too, am not immune to decision paralysis.

Some time ago, during the Covid-19 lockdown, my wife and I wanted to watch a Netflix series on our new Sony Smart TV. I spent almost an hour scanning Netflix and could not decide on a series we wanted to watch. I kept scrolling through all the options and my eyes oscillated constantly as I continued to try to choose the best series available on this streaming platform. In between, I browsed the internet, checked the IMDB ratings of some of the series and asked my wife about her recommendations. I also called my friends for their suggestions but still, I could not decide. After an hour of thorough analysis of multiple options available, I realized that the plethora of choices had paralyzed my ability to decide. In my quest to choose the perfect option, it was not just my fingers and eyes that bore the brunt of fatigue; there was cognitive fatigue, too.

Indecisiveness is pervasive. Everyone suffers from it.

Isn't it true that whenever we switch on our TV to listen to news debates, we struggle to stick to a particular channel, unless we are mesmerized by some boisterous anchor with fabulous looks? While assimilating every bit of information from the experts on TV, we always wonder, "Am I missing something here?" And it persistently prompts us to change frequency after frequency so that we can find more constructive and exciting content on other channels.

Day-to-day mundane decisions—choosing our perfect face wash out of the dozens that we hoard or deciding on a menu for breakfast or choosing the day's dress from our wardrobe—all consume our cognitive bandwidth in tremendous amounts. We end up wasting a considerable amount of time and energy while making these decisions.

The tragic part is that these decisions are ultimately insignificant as their impact on our life is marginal. Whether we have a Mexican burrito or we relish Greek salad or we savour Italian pasta, it serves the same purpose of momentarily satisfying our taste buds and quenching our appetite. Unless it is unhealthy or adulterated, the food does not impact us in a significant way. Similarly, whether we wear a black T-shirt with blue jeans or a formal shirt with trousers, it is immaterial except on the few occasions where a strict dress code is required. No one will look at us as obsessively as we do— standing in front of the mirror and deriving pleasure from our reflected image for countless hours.

Decision paralysis, incurred while making such trivial decisions, sucks our energy and hinders our ability to focus—often at the beginning of a beautiful day, eagerly waiting for us to show our natural brilliance.

INVESTIGATING DECISION PARALYSIS

The root cause for decision paralysis is: the quantum leap in the number of options and choices available to the consumer. It is death by many. You could also call it destruction by deluge. For example, there are 10 lakh restaurants listed on Zomato in India, with 10,000 of them located just in Delhi. In 1991, there was only one website on the internet. But now there are almost 1.5 billion websites. The proliferation of content and creators has been exponential. Similarly, if you visit any shopping mall, you'll find an infinite variety of attires with different patterns, designs and colors, causing a predicament and robbing a significant amount of your precious time as you make a choice.

Decision paralysis is bound to happen.

Research studies have proven that an increasing availability of choices is highly detrimental to our decision-making ability. In his book, *The Paradox of Choice: Why More Is Less*, American psychologist Barry Schwartz has highlighted how burgeoning choices are impacting the decision-making ability of consumers.

The concept of the *paradox of choices*, which Barry Schwartz propounded, was demonstrated in the seminal experiment conducted by psychologists Sheena Iyengar and Mark Lepper in 2000. In their experiment, shoppers at a food market were shown a display of 24 varieties of gourmet jam. The next day, only 6 varieties of jam were kept on display. They observed that although the 24 varieties on display attracted more customers' interest, people who saw the smaller display were 10 times more likely to buy the jam.

Jam is not the only entity that confounds shoppers, and shoppers are not the only category of people who are victims of drowning in this deluge of choices.

Imagine the situation of students. For any given subject, there exists a vast variety of reading material. Reference books, coaching academies notes, online platforms—all these options are putting enormous pressure on students to figure out the ideal and appropriate choice. As they try to analyze every available source to find comprehensive and relevant content, they inevitably suffer from decision-making paralysis.

TREATING DECISION PARALYSIS

Neurologists take a holistic approach to treating the limb paralysis of a stroke patient, including clot-dissolving drugs, nerve growth factors and extensive physiotherapy protocols. Similarly, I am offering you an omnibus remedy for treating your decision paralysis. The remedy is MDS: minimize, delegate and simplify. Strikingly potent! And yet I have not patented it and I'm dishing it out for zero cents to you.

Minimize

The most prudent approach to negotiating the current predicament—whether it's deciding on eatables from a supermarket, selecting apparel at a shopping mall, or choosing a book on a particular topic—is to adopt minimalism. Don't explore the galaxy of options fed and bombarded to your senses by the profit-making industries and fancy brands. They are just scurrying to influence your behavior through massive hoardings, posters and digital ads. Stick to only a few things and show immense faith in your decision. This will help you evade the debilitating effects of paralysis-by-analysis syndrome.

All epic luminaries minimize their possessions to maximize their decisiveness, productivity and happiness. Apple co-founder Steve Jobs always wore black mock turtlenecks, blue jeans and New Balance sneakers. When asked to share the reason for choosing a similar outfit each day, he said, "I don't want to waste my energy on this irrelevant process, as it allows me to save my precious morning time for important goals related to the firm." Famous physicist Albert Einstein also followed this strategy and bought several versions of his signature grey suit because he didn't want to fritter away his brainpower on deciding his attire every morning.

So, go and press the start button on minimalism and live a life filled with immortal joy, calm and no burden to clean up the mess around you. If you want to avoid the cognitive fatigue of multiple apps on your smartphone, you must minimize phone usage and delete the redundant apps. The same approach applies to the wardrobe. Refrain from putting excess stuff in your personal *almirah*. Keep only the bare essential clothing to reduce the time you spend standing in front of your wardrobe trying to decide on the dress to wear. Fewer choices lead to less fatigue.

Minimalism gives you another more tangible dividend: decluttering the environment around you and getting rid of unnecessary objects stimulates the focus and concentration required to work on the important goals in your life.

Delegate

It is irrational to fear delegating your decisions. You must start delegating trivial tasks to people around you—your peers, friends or family members. Some people are brilliant at making quick decisions. So why not let the other person decide on the meal to be ordered at a restaurant or suggest a dress that suits you? It automatically saves your energy, time and resources, which you can channel towards achieving your essential goals.

Simplify

Another structured and fruitful method to amplify your decision-making ability is to simplify. Streamline your short-term and long-term goals by formulating your itinerary in black and white. Your travel plans, social calendar (birthdays, marriages and other events that you are attending over the next year), books that you intend to read over the next six months, monthly grocery purchases, and the fitness schedule that you will follow over the next week. Write down everything in your personal notes.

If you don't execute this methodology, your overwhelming schedule can affect your mental bliss and internal joy. I started simplifying things very late in life. Now I realize, had I embraced it earlier (maybe 5-10 years back), I would have wasted less time and money, and lived a less convoluted life (with no compass to guide me to the right path). I had overweening enthusiasm and lived with a "do everything, try everything, and learn everything" attitude. I intentionally skipped the S in this MDS pill—until one day, when everything changed dramatically.

It was an evening I still remember vividly. I was running back after my calisthenics workout, and the weather was fantastic—absolutely pleasant, with gentle winds cooling my sweat and dissolving all my fatigue. But as I reached home and perched on my foyer sofa to have my post-workout recovery meal, I was angry at my wife because of this petty reason—my quinoa salad was missing beetroot. It was certainly not her fault; beetroot had been out of stock for a while. Both of us were to be blamed for not tracking our kitchen inventory. It was a time when we had a bevy of arguments and brawls over the silliest of things.

Ruffled by recurrent spats, I considered a permanent solution. I took one A4 sheet of paper and with my graphite pencil wrote, MUST KEEP EATABLES at the top, followed by a comprehensive list of everything, literally everything, that I wished to have in my kitchen. I then pasted it on the door of my refrigerator for daily vetting. This simple course correction not only amplified our decision-making when it came to purchasing groceries but also increased our household savings and fostered domestic peace, which we desired the most. No more bellowing at each other for things as tiny as peanuts, corn, lentils and flax seeds.

Now, let me teach you the way military people simplify their routine and maybe it will help you to emulate their drill and magnify your work output. Have you ever wondered why military leaders are considered efficient decision makers, even in the face of nerve-wracking battles and wars?

Raw courage is one thing but somewhere down the line, it is robustly linked with the way they begin their day before they cruise into their gladiatorial habitats. Their morning chores and rituals are substantially simplified. They don't have the luxury and liberty of keeping fancy beards—only a clean shave is applicable for them. Moreover, they are required to wear the same uniform every day and eat a fixed meal, collectively, in a common dining hall. This simple morning routine conserves their cerebral energy, which they use to take critical decisions during battle simulation drills.

Simplification is Amplification.

That's all about your MDS prescription. Use it profusely at home, in your work place, at food marts, or during travels and sabbaticals. Use it to not only augment your decisiveness but also multiply your economy, creativity and, most significant of all, your equanimity. And once you self-inoculate with MDS, you can begin thinking of building firmness towards your grandiose goals.

BUILDING FIRMNESS TOWARDS YOUR GOALS

Fundamentally, firmness is required at two vital stages of your goal journey.

Stage 1 is Initiation, the process of taking the first step towards the goal.

Stage 2 is Persistence, the process of pursuing your goal.

STAGE 1: INITIATION OF GOALS

When I was in school, our science teacher demonstrated an interesting experiment. He took a rupee one coin from his pocket and kept it at the center of a wooden table. He started his experiment by blowing air at the coin's edge to move it, but it did not move. The second time, he struck the coin with his middle finger and the coin fell to the floor. Then he stood at one corner of the table and tried to push the table with his fingers. The table did not move an inch until he pushed it with both hands.

He was teaching us Newton's First Law of Motion.

All objects have an inherent inertia of rest and tend to remain in that position unless acted upon by an unbalanced force. Some move by a light force, and some require a heavy push.

We, too, have in-built inertia that prevents us from taking the first step towards our goal.

INERTIAS

Inertia #1: Dilemma

Should I do it, or should I not? This is the classic dilemma that starts troubling us when we're about to start working on any lofty goal. But do you have any idea what dilemma does?

Dilemma creates deserters.

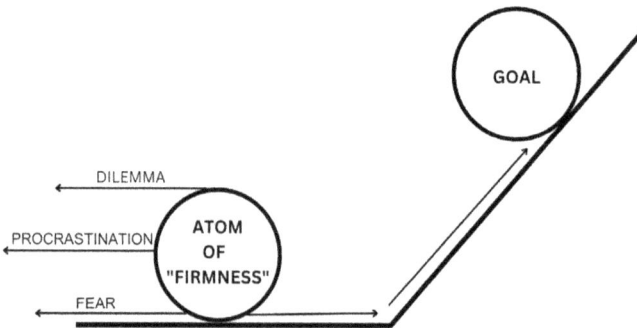

ATOM OF FIRMNESS AND THREE INERTIAS

The moment we spend a few days inside the zone of dilemma, we feel like abandoning our decisions altogether. A mind that resides perpetually in dilemma is bound to suffer from self-doubt, uncertainty and fear because it tends to perceive costs more than the benefits.

Dilemmas affect everyone. In the epic *Mahabharata*, the great warrior Arjuna also faced a dilemma about whether he should fight the army of his brothers, his great-grandfather and his Guru. His heart filled with compassion and his mind was worried about their grief and sufferings after the war. It was only when Lord Krishna convinced him that he would be establishing Dharma by defeating the Kauravas did he agree to fight the war.

Inertia #2: Procrastination

The harmful habit of postponing things sabotages our grandiose plans very covertly—not at all apparent to the naked eye. Procrastination is the enemy of destination. We don't begin work on most of our goals, believing that we'll start tomorrow. Even simple goals like cleaning the room and decluttering the environment, doing laundry, dishwashing or watering the saplings in our backyard, remain incomplete because we are unwilling to start.

And do you know who the mother of procrastination is?

It is your comfort zone!

We tend to defer difficult but important goals because we prefer to stay in a comfort bubble. We're always content with the status quo and never want to leave our bubble. Comfort kills our motivation to go for a morning fitness run, impedes our efforts to keep our room neat and tidy, or makes us disinclined to read transformative books or write creative blogs in our solitude hours.

Inertia #3: Fear

The fear of failure is a child born from the marriage between actions and attachment. Attachment to results creates undue anxiety about the prospective events, kills our focus, and hinders our ability to commit a hundred percent to our present actions. Thoughts of the future—"What will society think about me if I fail?"—accentuate our fear of failure. Such a negativity spiral keeps distracting us, brewing a tornado of self-doubt and pessimism in our minds.

Besides, every time we contemplate taking on challenging goals, our mind tends to recall past failures. To understand why this happens, you need to know this exciting concept of negativity bias, demonstrated lucidly by psychologist John Cacioppo. He conducted studies of participants who were shown pictures of either positive, negative or neutral images. His team of researchers observed that electric activity in the brain was more potent when participants were shown negative images, indicating more significant neural processing in the brain in response to negative stimuli. Past failures act as negative stimuli, which is why we recollect them so often. And every time we recollect, we get terrified and goals seems impossible to achieve.

This sums up the three inertias that keep us locked up in status quo.

Now let's explore the tool to break them.

BREAKING INERTIAS THROUGH THE GOAL PYRAMID

This goal pyramid highlights certain essential steps in sequence, and each step generates a powerful force to break the inertia discussed in the previous section.

INERTIAS

TO ELIMINATE
DETACH → FEAR

TO BEAT
START → PROCRASTINATION

TO RESOLVE
ANALYZE → DILEMMA

GOAL PYRAMID

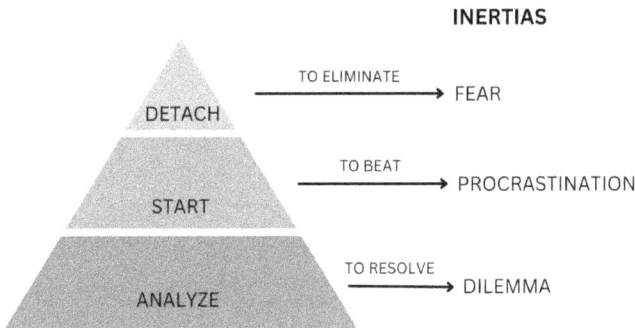

Step 1: Analyze

Analysis is the first step to resolve all dilemmas. And there is a time-tested approach to do this: CBA or Cost-Benefit Analysis. Remember that every decision has its benefits as well as costs. For example, pursuing a career in sports ensures our physical and mental well-being and teaches us many values like discipline, courage, patience and perseverance. Plus, it provides a unique opportunity to earn accolades and laurels for our country. However, it also involves certain costs such as the risk of permanent injuries, sacrificing premium family time, and missing the jovial company of close friends.

Unfortunately, when we do CBA, most of us get trapped in the negativity bias and tend to perceive adverse outcomes even before we embark on our goals.

Sagacity lies in keeping a distance from this sort of a negative disposition. Do not end up using CBA as a fear-mongering tool. Instead, it should be leveraged to cultivate a positive frame of mind. This tool is effective only when it is used in a pragmatic as well as an optimistic manner.

Step 2: Start

Once you analyze and decide, the next course of action is to start. It is the perfect antidote for the inertia of procrastination. The primary reason we postpone most essential goals is that we're internally hesitant to begin. Whether it is the goal of learning a musical instrument, reading a non-fiction book, or investing in the stock market—the trick is to get started. We wait for the right time and an auspicious occasion to take any significant decision. But the searing fact is that the right time never arrives, and we never get to see the auspicious occasion. We perpetually harbor this feeling that we're not adequately qualified to start on big goals, but the universal truth is that we'll never be qualified to start. So don't wait for anything special to happen. Just START!

I follow a 10-seconds rule to break my inertia. Whether it is doing 100 push-ups upon waking up every morning, making my bed and folding my mosquito net, keeping my table clean, penning down fresh thoughts in my writing journal, taking my pet for a morning walk, or washing my sports gear. Even if it seems difficult or I feel disinclined to do it, I don't take more than 10 seconds to start once I have thought about doing it. And when I begin, it becomes pretty easy. Thoughts and actions are like a couple in love. Lesser the distance, stronger is the union.

There are numerous self-help books in stores recommending different times within which you should commence a task. Some suggest 5 seconds, some say 60 seconds, while others propound 2 minutes. But as 10 seconds works for me, I follow this. You can decide it based on what works for you. Yet my earnest advice is to not keep it too long, otherwise you'd be risking putting your ideas in suspended animation forever, and enforcing a life-long embargo on the ignition of your sparks.

In the medical profession, us doctors stick to a 'golden hour' principle to salvage the life of a patient—we have to act within 60 minutes to render the necessary resuscitation. If we don't do it, all vital organs—heart, brain, kidney and lungs—would stop functioning and we might lose the patient.

What is your 'golden seconds' commandment?

Decide it and implement it every single time you find it demanding to start a task. And as you know, just as a rocket has a limited window of time to gain escape velocity and reach its orbit, you, too, have a narrow window to launch yourself into the trajectory of achievers. If you don't act within this perform-or-perish time slot, *you will fail to take off*, just like the thousands of space missions that meet tragic ends every year.

Step 3: Detach

After making a gorgeous start, the third step, which is monumentally essential and which is an ultimate remedy for the fear of failure, is detachment.

What is detachment after all?

In the *Bhagavad Gita*, Lord Krishna tells Arjuna that acting with detachment means doing the right thing because it needs to be done without worrying about success or failure. I think this summarizes everything.

Too much attachment to outcomes and a sickly obsession with rewards triggers unnecessary stress and tension about events that are unlikely to happen. Most athletes fail to deliver on the big stage because their focus is on the expectations, awards and acclaim, rather than on their elite training. A multitude of start-ups are buried at the initial stage because entrepreneurs start dreaming prematurely about making their enterprise the next big thing instead of revamping their existing processes. They are not detached.

One practical way to forego detachment is to break down your goals into short-term targets and manageable tasks; take it as an opportunity to learn and grow and enjoy the journey as you commute ahead.

So far, we have discussed building firmness while embarking on our goals. But the buck does not stop here. Firmness is also required in persisting with our goals.

STAGE 2: PERSISTENCE WITH GOALS

Dr Schwartz correctly figured out that the availability of choices not only results in decision paralysis but also leads to dissatisfaction after you succeed in making a decision. There is always residual regret and unhappiness even after selecting the best option available. This dissatisfaction breeds a tendency to seek fresh alternatives and drives people to change one decision after another, such as switching to a different smartphone or exploring a new career.

That is why the second stage of firmness is so essential. While embarking on any big goal, merely taking the first bold step does not predict your success. Instead, it is the unrelenting resolve and firm conviction for your goal that determines eventual glory.

All legendary achievers have one thing in common: a singular focus and extreme obsession with their coveted dream, and their tendency not to capitulate despite repeated failures. Elon Musk has succeeded in building Space X, a phenomenal company, amid a flurry of detractors and massive failures in the past. He has achieved it because he had the firm conviction to persist with his decision to venture into the domain that no one ever dared to tread before. He is still driven by tremendous belief in his idea to make Mars an inhabitable planet.

Persisting with goals requires a unique blend of profound patience, unwavering grit and unyielding stubbornness. Ultimately, it boils down to whether you behave like a pillar or a pendulum.

PILLAR VS. PENDULUM

In 2016, I visited Limerick, the second largest city in the Republic of Ireland, to participate in the World Medical Games and Symposium. It had been a hectic week and I was physically exhausted after competing in back-to-back athletic events. So, I decided to relax. A day before my return flight to New Delhi, I booked a tourist bus to visit Galway Beach—the place the hotel receptionist had strongly recommended when I asked her about a must-see destination nearby.

As our coach was about to depart, I noticed a tall blonde hurriedly boarding it. She came and sat right next to me. She was attractive and I surreptitiously looked at her blonde hair and long legs as she adjusted herself in the compact space in her seat, spreading her right leg partially into the aisle, which bisected the bus into two compartments. My head reflexively turned to the window on my left as the strong scent of her perfume struck me.

"Hello, I am Annie from the States," she said with a soft smile as I turned to look at her.

Intrigued by what she meant by the States, I reciprocated with my introduction. I soon realized that she meant the United States of America.

On the way to our destination, we had a candid conversation. She was on a three-month sabbatical to Europe and Asia. I learnt that she was a Geography teacher and she described the geological processes responsible for the Karst topography of the region running parallel to us. During a brief halt en route, we strolled along the gorgeous caves, sinkholes and ground streams. And the way she explained the process of limestone rocks dissolving and disintegrating to make these exquisite features was simply enlightening. Her erudition overshadowed her elegance.

We finally reached the rugged cliffs of Galway, which offered a breathtaking view of the beautiful Atlantic coast. The surrounding vast swath of water reminded me of *The Rime of the Ancient Mariner:* "Water, water, every where,/And all the boards did shrink;/Water, water, every where,/Nor any drop to drink."

After de-boarding, we followed the crowd and went straight to the reception to purchase tickets for the sand trail on the cliff along the coast, overlooking the massive ocean. While walking on this long and narrow trail, Annie and I barely managed to anchor ourselves against the gusty coastal winds. When we stopped and steadied ourselves to observe the beautiful horizon, Annie noticed a solitary pillar at a short distance from us. She intently observed the pillar, while still oscillating due to the thrust of the turbulent winds. The next moment, she turned to me and surprised me with a question, "Dear, don't you think that we should behave more like a pillar and less like a pendulum?"

I found her statement confounding.

Gauging my bewildered look, she only replied, "Look at the pillar! Amid the ferocious winds, it is standing strong and erect, unlike us, oscillating like a pendulum." She continued, "No matter how turbulent and windy the circumstances are, we should also act like that pillar and remain firm in our goals, instead of behaving like a pendulum, moving from one trivial goal to another."

I have always been grateful to Annie for teaching me this life-changing lesson. Whenever my firmness has dwindled since, her lesson has always helped me to wield focus and conviction.

You have a choice. Either you can opt to act as a strong pillar that remains firm in its position, or you can act like a pendulum, swinging from one position to another.

KEEPING YOUR PILLAR SAFE FROM 4D ELEMENTS

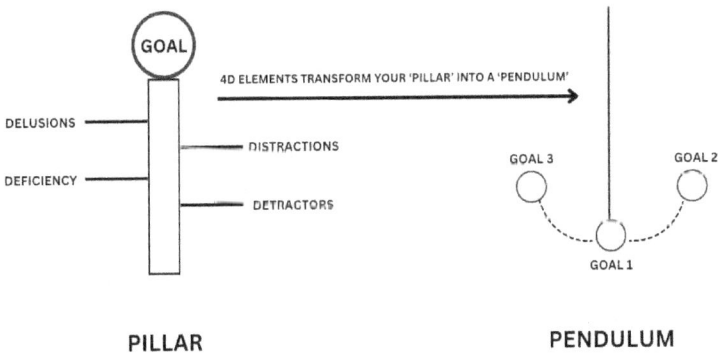

PILLAR   PENDULUM

There are 4 elements, I call them the 4D elements, that are the biggest threats to your goal pillar. If you nurture these elements, they will covertly corrode your pillar's foundation and force you to follow a pendulum's trajectory, drifting from one goal to another.

So, it is necessary to discuss these threats.

Element #1: Distractions

In today's age of technology and expanding social media, it's not difficult to encounter people who somehow manage to intrude into your personal life through platforms like WhatsApp, Instagram or Facebook. Very soon, they become your friends and send irrelevant messages or ask your company for unnecessary outings to kill their time. Just ignore them. Do not worry that you'll lose these friends if you don't entertain them, or that you will disappoint them and hurt their expectations and feelings if you don't oblige.

Firmness in saying an emphatic NO to annoying people, and to the things that are irrelevant to your ambition and happiness, is a proven strategy to anchor discipline. Be cautious of your relatives, too. It is not uncommon to find some uncles, aunts and cousins who keep pestering you to attend every family function. If you're sacrificing your sanctified priorities to attend their holy events, you're making a wrong decision in acceding to their requests. Be firm in simply saying a big NO. And let me tell you honestly— all these relatives who express their anger for not attending their functions will start singing your praises once you succeed. After you accomplish your set goals, the same people who earlier complained to your parents that you were rebuffing their invitations, will become emissaries of your efforts and sacrifices.

The other day, while I listened to the insightful podcast *Think Fast, Talk Smart* by Matt Abrahams, I apprehended the real difference between a faint-hearted NO and a robust NO. I discovered the hidden power of giving a clear and firm response in situations that force us to think in extremes and leave us uncertain. Matt had invited an ace speaker on the show who illustrated how the words we choose can have a profound impact on our intentions and behavior. That session minted a priceless pearl of wisdom for me, "Switch I *can't* with I *don't* to make phenomenal gains."

Next time, when someone offers sweets heavily loaded with white poison to you, don't say, "I can't eat," say, "I don't eat," and trust me you won't have any regret of not tasting it, no lingering craving. Or if your pals ask you to join them for the nightclub party, don't say, "I can't go," or "I need to study." Staunchly say, "I don't go," and believe me, you won't repent missing the parties. When someone approaches you for undue favors or forces you to accept a bribe, don't respond with, "I can't do it." Instead reply with the enormous conviction, "I don't do such wicked things."

Keeping your citadel of sovereign thinking secured from hostile forces will prevent you from giving in to such tempting moments. Don't you think that things like sugar, high decibel nightclubs and corruption are toxic distractions on the way to your goals—whether they're physical, professional or spiritual? Certainly, yes!

Learning to say a robust NO is an effective way to ward off all vile distractions.

Element #2: Delusions

Fame, money and power are such monstrous delusions that even if you're doing remarkably well in something, they'll always tempt you to tread the wrong path.

Don't live in a delusional world when comparing your decisions vis-a-vis others. The feeling that their smartphone is better than yours, or the assumption that their job is more relaxing and offers better perks and privileges, yields nothing. It only sucks your inner peace. Don't be a victim of the illusion that the grass is always greener on the other side because the brutal reality is that those who are on the other side, too, see the grass on your side as being greener.

I have an anecdote to share that will illustrate how delusions are mighty dream destroyers.

It's about Raghuveer, a tall and charismatic lad in my village. He's not exactly my close friend but I know him as we studied at the same primary school. Until a few years back, he was doing very well—he had become a prominent land baron and I must give him apt credit for transforming the agricultural economy of my village. He had invested heavily in developing the post-harvest infrastructure—warehouses, cold storages and processing clusters—and had made significant profits by selling packaged millets and vegetables in the urban marketplace.

But since he had a magnetic personality, he decided to become an actor and went to Mumbai in hot pursuit of his pipe dream. However, much to his chagrin, he was completely shocked to discover that it was not just flamboyance that made actors out of small-town guys. Instead, Bollywood was looking for the true aficionados and their unquenching appetite for acting in its future superstars. He wanted to become the heartthrob of the nation overnight, the likes of Shah Rukh Khan, Big B and Hrithik Roshan. But he didn't realize that to become their kind, he had to act better than their kind; that to thrive, he shouldn't try to become their doppelgänger, and instead highlight his originality and carve his own niche. As Robin Sharma, my favorite author, puts it so succinctly in *The Wealth Money Can't Buy*: "You can copy your heroes or you can influence your industry, but you'll never be able to do both."

Raghuveer was duped by the glamour and glitter of Page 3 stories and the faux eminence sold by the biased media. When he arrived in Mumbai, what he witnessed was poles apart from what he had visualized in his fantasy world. A perfect delusion. Life here is not romantic at all, as the movies portray to us so vividly. It is frenetic. Every day, denizens of the town scramble to board the local trains, jostle to find a decent space to stand and commute, and reach their offices with lunchboxes and satchels to work unremittingly. Life runs faster than the speed of light.

Living in a tiny rented 1 BHK, spurred by the gigantic ambition to make a towering name and fame for himself, Raghuveer would travel across the city every day for dozens of studio auditions. He was not the only one in this mad race; there were truckloads of others, more handsome and talented than him, standing in queue to showcase their prowess. "I couldn't sleep sometimes. It was so tormenting," he admitted during an honest conversation when I met him last year. "Because as you know, the work culture in the film city is all about working non-stop till sunrise. It's staggering competitiveness. If you don't have the fortitude and patience to hang in there, you'd probably hang yourself," he had recounted his horrors in a ruffled voice.

He felt as if the pressure of performance had smothered his passion, and murdered his instincts to persist in that crammed up, distressing environment. He lived in dread. His wretched state reminded me of this Japanese proverb: "Vision without action is a daydream. Action without vision is a nightmare." It happens when you prepare for yourself a deadly mélange of 95% ambition and 5% aptitude. A poisonous recipe to kill all your dreams. Broken and crushed, he forsook his aspirations and stuffed his beige suitcase with all his personal belongings to return to his hometown.

Can you fathom why Raghuveer met with this misadventure?

It's simple. He made a mistake by following the delusional model of goal-setting. Acting was not his caliber; it was not in his blood. He had a flamboyant body with killer looks, perfect anatomy in every muscle and vein. But he lacked one indispensable element: he wasn't a splashy artist. To survive in Bollywood and get noticed by movie makers, you have to be a damn good artist, and on top of it, possess an insatiable hunger for daily incremental improvements in your craft.

In every village, town or city, there are thousands like Raghuveer who operate like misguided missiles and navigate aimlessly with no realistic target. And then they crash-land in some barren field, extinguishing their burning desires and the brio that they were born with. Eventually, they withdraw from all challenging pursuits and retire to become wise saints selling philosophy to the next generation. Do you really want that to happen to you? I guess you don't.

So don't let delusions (fame, money, power) affect your trajectory and change the fabulous goals that you've chosen after P2P. You would be betraying the talents you have been gifted with and the values that you adore and espouse.

Element #3: Detractors

It is a sad truth that you will always find more detractors than actors around you, detractors who relentlessly condemn your bold steps and label you things like a maniac or paranoid. And detractors exist everywhere—among your friends, enemies and family, too. They shower you with unwarranted wisdom about life decisions, as if they possess a supernatural power to segregate good decisions from bad ones. You don't need to listen to them. Fortify your goal pillar with a soundproof layer to deflect such discouraging voices.

Let me share my story with you. A few months ago, just before I finished this book, I started a fitness challenge on one of the WhatsApp groups: "Six-packs in sixty days." Yes, six-pack abs! In quest of my sacred goal, I sweated profusely and followed a disciplined diet focused on simple, healthy, balanced food. In this journey, I met a few people who made galling comments like, "Sanjeev, you look emaciated. Cachexic. Skinny. Like a TB patient. What has happened to you? I hope all is well?" Or, "Buddy, six-packs are a massive fraud. A frantic race. Absolutely not healthy at all. And not sustainable, too, in the long term. Why are you doing it?" I found it despicable.

Of course, it's true that I lost 10-12 kg of body weight over those 60 days, and my body fat percentage plunged sharply from 14 % to 7%. But to win something, you have to lose something. Life is a zero-sum game. Isn't it? For me, my loss was my body fat, but my win was my conspicuous abs.

If you want to shine like the sun, you need to burn like the sun. Nothing comes free of cost. Lord Gautam Buddha went through an extended ordeal when he sat for 49 days under the sacred fig tree, without any food or water, to attain his goal of Enlightenment. My goal was to develop a six-pack. It was my Nirvana.

This whole process wasn't just a physical journey, it was a spiritual pilgrimage too. It taught me how avoiding impulsive eating is so beneficial in micromanaging our emotions at a granular level, and how deeply it impacts the way we think, act and behave. It made me calmer, patient, tolerant, content, resilient, energetic, productive, confident, and a battery of other bonuses. It was my Nalanda—a perfect university for learning the highest and noblest of premium virtues. Absolutely enriching and ethereal!

And if you, too, are seeking spiritualism, I have an important message for you: you don't need to go to Mecca, Rome, Ayodhya or Jerusalem to discover providence, to connect to your inner self or the Supreme Being. If you optimize the way you exercise, eat and live, you will realize God.

This was my fitness goal.

What is your fitness goal? Or any other goal that, when achieved, would make you attain Nirvana? No matter how weird or bohemian it is—learning Bachata dance, immersing yourself in an ice bath for hours, practicing meditative chanting for days and days like monks, spending a complete day every month at an orphanage, or doing adventurous activities such as bungee jumping and solo sky diving. Identify it and then commit one hundred percent and stick to it, even in the face of a full brigade of detractors.

Element #4: Deficiency

The euphoria that we experience after we get a desired entity declines steadily after the initial gratification subsides—whether it is a shiny Porsche, a shimmering gem stone, or a sea-facing apartment. Deficiency is universal. And it is a dangerous malady because it starts an unending process to acquire and hoard a bunch of new things that are slated to end up in obsolescence.

It is the same with goals. The exuberance we feel after we have achieved our goals is momentary, and inevitably gives way to a feeling of scarcity. We achieve big results but then we fail to sustain the momentum because we're not satisfied and content with what we've achieved. We hit an 8% body fat percentage with a strict dietary and exercise routine, but when we watch our friends and family members gulping down burgers, pizzas, pastas, and other fast food, we feel that we're missing out on something. We wonder, "Why should I make sacrifices? I only have one life. So why not enjoy every amazing flavor available to me?" This sense of inadequacy wipes away all the hard work and we are back to zero.

For another example, we study for six to eight hours a day for plenty of weeks, but when we see our colleagues going to parties and movies, we feel deprived and become part of the legion. We crack the IIT exams but the ecstasy slowly fades as life returns to normal after a few days. Although we enter college with many lofty aspirations, many among us don't find engineering an exciting prospect after a while. This feeling of deficiency pushes us to abandon engineering and motivates us to become big-time entrepreneurs, civil servants and top-notch managers. Some who're driven by passion and strong beliefs do very well. However, those who are victims of a fickle mindset change their decisions frequently, and eventually fail to deliver concrete results in their new ventures.

The scientific explanation for this pervasive deficiency is worth studying. The fact is that dopamine secreting pathways reach saturation after a particular time, and basal dopamine levels in the blood deplete, starting the process to seek something fresh that can secrete additional dopamine and is more rewarding. The brain of a Homo sapien is never satisfied. It is sensible to seek dopamine shots by surpassing difficult milestones that you set on the way to your goals. But it is absolutely foolhardy to seek dopamine from impulsive explorations into fields that are not inherently yours and pursuing goals that are not in sync with your genius. That is a recipe for guaranteed disaster. Isn't it?

The panacea for this sense of deficiency is to develop a tubular vision. You need to put on imaginary spectacles to obstruct your lateral field of view and ignore what is happening at the periphery. Ignore what others are chasing, how they commute, how many material possessions they're hoarding, or how many acres of property they hold. Just look straight and keep moving ahead.

To sum up, it is critical that you bulletproof your pillar against these four elements during the second stage of firmness. This is more essential because no matter how much boldness you demonstrate at the beginning, if you don't persist with your goal, it will ruin your prospects of success.

Takeaways

- Firmness is essential during two vital stages of your goal journey. Stage 1 is Initiation, taking the first step towards your goals. Stage 2 is Persistence, the process of pursuing your goals.

- To cultivate firmness in initiating goals, seek the help of a goal pyramid, which highlights a step-by-step process to arrive at a firm decision.

- To leverage firmness in persisting with your goals, you must behave like a pillar and not a pendulum.

- Keep your pillar safe from 4D elements—delusions, distractions, detractors and deficiency.

PENCIL WORK

- Draw a pillar and on the top of it, enumerate one goal that is most dear to you, which you always dream of achieving. And then list 4Ds beside it.

- Now, endorse your sacred pledge: "I'll always think about, work towards, and live with this singular goal, no matter how hard I'm hit by a barrage of 4Ds."

STEP 3: **ENDURE**

ATOM 2

FLEXIBILITY

'Blessed are the flexible, for they will not allow themselves to become bent out of shape!'

– Robert Ludlum

CHAPTER 5

Flexibility

'The Second Atom' of the Graphene Mentality

What you will learn in this chapter

- How flexibility enables you to endure through challenges and a hostile atmosphere.
- How flexibility in certain essentials of life—sleep, food, work and family—is critical to the accomplishment of your goals.

It may seem contradictory to advocate for both firmness and flexibility as part of The Graphene Mentality. But they can coexist. Think about the element graphene. It is firm as well as flexible. In addition to firmness, flexibility makes it a wonder element worthy of being successfully used in different industries.

Similarly, if you want to accomplish your goals and be successful, you must demonstrate flexibility, regardless of how firm and stubborn you are.

To illustrate, let me narrate how I leveraged flexibility to realize my desired goal of becoming a paratrooper. The reason I set this goal was not just that I was fascinated by the charm of the maroon beret—a privilege that differentiates paratroopers from others in the army. My real purpose was to challenge myself by living their perilous and thrilling life. I desperately wanted to be a member of this elite league.

Therefore, in 2011, I volunteered for the probation, a grueling period of 30 days during which willing candidates are screened for certain qualities necessary for becoming a paratrooper. I was exposed to harsh living conditions and had access to only limited foods, which included edible plants, insects and even stray animals. I ate grasshoppers, frogs, dogs, ducks, and even snakes. It might sound weird (might be unethical, too), but I had to do all this to maintain steady glucose levels around the clock and deliver a fatigue-free performance. When your energy is depleted, and you must walk 25 km with heavy backpacks, won't you eat everything, including grasshoppers? Yes, you will! If your hunger for reaching your objective overpowers you more than anything else, you'll eat everything (including grasshoppers) to energize yourself to march forward.

I was also forced to eat glass—not that my instructor was crazy but because he wanted to assess whether I was fit and flexible enough to join their legion. Para Commandos are popularly called Glass Eaters because they don't consider their drink finished until the last few drops of Old Monk that are stuck on the inner surface of the glass, are also gulped down. Counterintuitively, eating glass is not an unhealthy ritual for them, as the glass, when crushed into a powder, is a rich source of silica and can be swallowed comfortably.

Besides food, I had to be flexible with my sleep as well. I slept outdoors in makeshift tents and my biological clock went haywire, as there was no certainty of getting fixed hours of sleep. Sometimes, I slept just 2-3 hours to remain awake to ensure the security of my campsite. My instructor also gave me some exciting nighttime assignments, such as finding the oldest grave in the graveyard, proposing to any random girl with my naked body wrapped in twigs and leaves, or checking whether the sentry of the garrison was awake. Over time, I adapted to sleep disruptions fabulously, and it made my biological clock so robust and automated that I did not need an alarm clock to wake me up.

My flexibility was tested in other domains as well. One such thing was cohabiting with unfamiliar faces hailing from diverse regions with different ideologies, languages and ethnicities. When we dwelled inside the four walls of nondescript, camouflaged canvas, we found that embracing each other's views and thoughts was the only key to harmony and brotherhood.

Physical training was another aspect that tested my flexibility to the core. During bursts of rigorous training in hostile terrains, with a bare essential amount of water permitted for hydration, it was only my physical and mental flexibility that helped me to endure. Like the hippopotamus adapts itself to an aquatic habitat by keeping its eyes, ears and nostrils high above the head so that it can see, hear and breathe, I, too, adapted to the environment for my survival.

In essence, flexibility was the passport that facilitated my travel through the rigors of probation and enabled me to accomplish my goal of earning the prestigious maroon beret.

Now, the ultimate germane question: how can YOU exploit flexibility to achieve your goals?

EXPLOITING FLEXIBILITY TO ACHIEVE YOUR GOALS

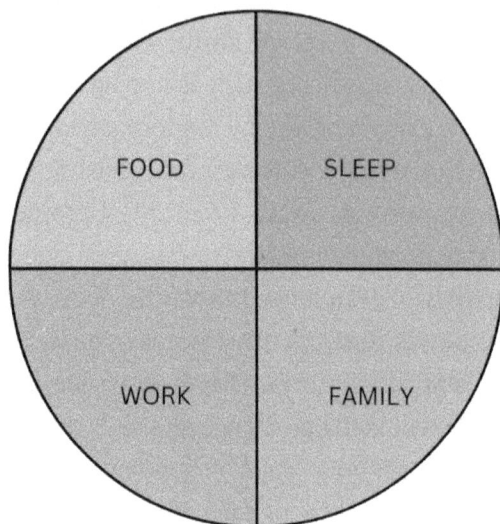

ATOM OF FLEXIBILITY

The Flexibility Quotient (FQ) in these essential aspects of your life—food, sleep, work and family—is strongly related to the accomplishment of your personal goals. Although there are many other dimensions of our lives which require a flexible approach, these four remain the vital few that profoundly intersect with our goal prospects. Let's discuss the relevance of FQ in each segment.

A. FOOD

We are extremely rigid regarding our food choices and crave specific dishes, particularly the delicious ones heavily loaded with salt or sugar. It is difficult to change our genetically wired taste buds and strongly conditioned food habits.

But it's not our fault. Salt and sugar became an intrinsic part of our diet because they provided an evolutionary advantage to our ancestors by enhancing their chances of survival while they lived nomadic lives. It worked in two ways. One, it helped them build the energy reserves required for manual labor and long hours on their feet. Two, it allowed them to fight starvation due to floods, drought and famines, which were quite frequent in those days. Over time, the intake of these ingredients intensified, and the behavior was transmitted through the generations, resulting in the significant conditioning of our minds to crave more of the same.

However, times have changed, and salt and sugar don't have survival benefits any more. They are just the post-workout recovery agents for athletes. Besides, if taken in excess, they act as poisons, causing ailments like hypertension, obesity and diabetes. So, there is no wisdom in rigidly sticking to salt and sugar because we have plenty of other healthy options in the market that were unavailable during the Stone Age.

When our ancestors wandered in the wilderness and scrambled for food, they had only one goal: to survive and fight. Like our forefathers, we are also constantly wandering from one location to another in pursuit of our goals. Some are commuting for business, some for education and employment, some for spiritual enlightenment, and many others for sports. And wherever we go, we have access to numerous cuisines, different from our staple diets, to which our taste buds are not accustomed. Amid these circumstances, being flexible in our food choices not only helps us survive but also enhances our performance. Let's explore how it does that.

Neeraj Chopra is an ace athlete who became the first ever Indian to win an Olympic gold in the javelin throw during the 2020 Tokyo Olympics (and he repeated his scintillating performance by winning a silver medal in the 2024 Paris Olympics). Since he was a child, he has been a strict vegetarian, and his diet comprised roti, vegetables, fruits, milk and *churma* (a sweet delicacy from Haryana). However, in 2016, circumstances forced him to begin eating non-vegetarian food. He was in Portland, USA, for a training camp when he realized he was gradually losing weight. And with not many vegetarian options around him, he had to eat eggs and grilled chicken breasts as a source of protein. After that, these foods became an integral part of his dietary regimen and helped him increase his muscle mass and strength considerably, allowing him to throw the javelin further and further.

To cut a long story short, besides his flexible body, it was his flexible decision to start eating chicken and eggs that powered him for the historic 87.78 meter throw in Tokyo that fetched him the Olympic gold.

Through this anecdote, I'm not advocating that you should become a non-vegetarian and stop eating a vegetarian diet. The message is simple. Whatever segment you belong to, whether you're a student, an entrepreneur, a doctor, an engineer, a teacher, a scientist, or a sportsperson, you will often travel to places where your favorite foods won't be available. Embracing local cuisines will not only keep you satiated and happy, but it will also provide sufficient energy to augment your productivity.

There is another aspect of food where you must show flexibility. It has to do with the elimination of the daily impulse to fill your stomach. Start fasting once every week. It has numerous benefits: detoxification of your digestive system, better overall mood, more working energy, and improvement in your average life span. Researchers have found that ensuring a complete rest for the digestive system protects telomeres—the end caps on your DNA—and prevents its degradation, thus slowing the aging process.

B. SLEEP

Be flexible with your sleep.

Getting seven to eight hours of healthy sleep, which experts recommend, is unarguably a productive strategy that ensures adequate recovery, repair and growth of your cells and tissues. However, circumstances are not so favorable every night that you can sleep peacefully, in a calm and serene environment, for seven to eight hours. Certain things are not in your control. Your sleep could be interrupted by loud music from your neighbor's house, the crankiness of the construction machinery, the persistent snoring of the person sleeping next to you, the continuous cry of your own kid or even random uninvited negative thoughts before an important day.

You must be able to adapt to such inadvertent disruptions and refrain from blaming them if you are not able to deliver. No matter how fatigued, irritated or distracted you are in the morning, it is an agonizing reality that everyone will expect a spectacular show from you. People just don't care enough to dig into the fact that your sleep was disrupted the night before, and that it is hindering your ability to perform at the peak of your potential.

In the previous section, we discussed how flexibility helped star athlete Neeraj Chopra achieve his goal. Now, let us see how Abhinav Bindra, the only person other than Neeraj who has ever won an Olympic gold for India, demonstrated flexibility and accomplished his goal. He is a prolific shooter who won the gold in the 10-meter Air Rifle finals at the 2008 Beijing Olympics. We can all remember the image of the Indian flag rising proudly to the tune of our national anthem. But few of us know what he went through before the day. "The night before the gold medal haul, I had panic attacks. I could barely sleep. I accepted the situation and absorbed the pressure, enduring it and working with it," Bindra conceded after winning the medal.

The big learning point in Bindra's story is that, despite a turbulent night before his main event, he was flexible enough to endure it calmly, which allowed him to shoot with precision and achieve his goal. The process of goal attainment demands a flexible sleep schedule, even though most people don't recommend it and find it unhealthy, adversely affecting memory and mood.

Again, to illustrate why a flexible sleep schedule is so vital, let me share how it assisted my wife in pursuing one of her goals.

At the outset, ever since I met her, she was very rigid regarding her sleep—she slept for at least 10 hours every day, and followed it with fierce discipline. But that changed on September 27, 2021, the day our little gem Viraj was born. After this day, her routine changed drastically and her circadian rhythm was completely disrupted. It was really tough for her, especially in the initial six months when she had multiple obligations—intermittent breastfeeding, frequent diaper changes, consoling intractable cries, and attending to phone calls by relatives who enquired about the baby's health. Compounding her woes was postpartum depression because of hormonal changes, resulting in frequent bouts of mood swings.

But she activated her atom of flexibility and gradually adapted her sleep schedule, tuning it to the child's needs and requirements. A three-month-old baby cannot change his sleeping pattern, nor can you train him. It is the mother who has to adjust accordingly. Her only goal during this critical phase was to ensure optimum growth and development of her child through proper nutrition and timely care. And she could fulfill her goal because she was flexible about her sleep schedule. When the goal is as selfless and pious as feeding and caring for your child, no element can impede your efforts, let alone sleep disruptions.

C. WORK

To carve out success in your professional goals, work is the third essential domain of your life where you need to be flexible. Primarily, this flexibility is required in two chief aspects of your work—your work schedule and your workplace.

Work schedule

It is not uncommon to see people around us who are perpetually obsessed with pending work and are always overwhelmed by the stress of meeting their professional goals. If you're one of them, the only pragmatic advice that I can give you, and that has supported me in my journey so far, is this:

Be flexible with the work hours that you target every day. You need not imitate anyone in this aspect. Do not compare yourself with the person working 16 hours a day. Quality matters more than quantity and consistent work is more productive than a single burst of intense work. If you are working 6-8 hours per day and persist with this schedule daily, you will reap more benefits than by working for 16 hours a day in an inconsistent manner. A prolonged and exhaustive work session in a frantic mode invariably leads to a steep fall in enthusiasm the next day due to over-saturation.

One more take-home principle. While you're working, it does not matter whether you're in the habit of working late at night or you like to work in the early hours of the morning. Choose a time that is comfortable to you, a time when you don't feel distracted, and when your concentration and attention are at their peak.

Workplace

Flexibility at your workplace is a sure shot license to smooth growth and prosperity in your career. But adapting to an unfamiliar environment is not an easy job, just like it is not easy for an exotic plant to anchor its roots in a new place with uncongenial soil, nutrients and water levels.

But let's imagine a situation: what if we could become a mystic plant, one that can survive all climate and topographic conditions? What if we could metamorphose into a cactus when in the desert, into a rhododendron when in the inhospitable peaks of the Himalayas, and into a mangrove when put in marshy wetlands?

How incredible would that be?

Adaptation is the only silver bullet to live, thrive, perform, grow and prosper in all ecosystems. When you live in Rome, you should be willing to do as the Romans do; if you're in Mongolia, live as the Mongolians live; and if you're in Australia, work as the Australians work. That is the fundamental modus operandi of existence and survival, isn't it?

When I graduated from secondary school and entered college for the first time, the new environment was a complete cultural shock. During our inaugural address, I was sitting along with students from North, East, West and South India, who spoke different languages and dialects, and believed in their own Gods, mythology and legends. And yet we had congregated at that auspicious lecture hall for a common purpose that would bind us for the next five odd years. While I sat there, I rued leaving my school days, my adorable friends and their unconditional love, and the consummate friendship that we had built together over seven years.

But the next moment, our warden (what a lean, smart, flamboyant fatherly figure he was to all of us) walked up to the stage, illuminated the hall with his mentoring torch and uttered these life-changing words: "My dear young guns, you're the chosen ones. And that's the precise reason you're sitting here in this august gathering, having accomplished dreams that you visualized in your sprouting age. Since you will be embarking on your second life very soon, I have an important message. In fact, not a message, a guiding edict for you all: emerge from your cocoons and shells and induct yourself into this massive yet magnificent amphitheater, where you will be spending the best five years of your life. Be gregarious. Interact fully. Make friends. Enjoy together. Learn collectively. Meet the love of your life. Unleash your slumbering talents and extravagant gifts. And if you do this, I guarantee you will be the mightiest Spartans when you leave this arena."

And indeed, he was right. When we graduated, we were brimming with a warrior's mentality, ready to conquer mountainous heights and seemingly impossible possibilities.

Do you get what our warden was trying to convey to us?

He was highlighting the necessity of the flexibility that we needed to develop in our new battlefield. And I would suggest that you, too, obey the same guiding edict in your life as you travel to novel places and meet unknown people. If you intend to build a strong peer group, you must discard timidity while making new friends. You ought to shed your inner hesitation of opening yourself to the outside world. I agree that old friends are trustworthy, that they help identify your strengths and weaknesses, and that they render unflinching support during crises and allow you to live a fulfilling and cheerful life.

However, the new friends that you'd be making belong to a diverse pool with a variety of attributes, attitudes and beliefs, which will broaden your perspective in life as you share their insights and knowledge. Though they might not provide you with the same intimacy and bonding as your old friends do, they'll certainly push you to grow in a significant manner. After all, isn't growing in life as essential as living?

Besides ensuring your personal and career growth, flexibility at your workplace will also help you to deal with new challenges. Your work atmosphere may often be stressful and a lot more different from home, school or your neighborhood. You might have been coddled by your parents in your formative years but you must shed that skin and be formidable once you enter the professional orbit.

Colleagues at your workplace are not like your college mates. They are remarkably different in their character and motives. Some are opportunists, some are careerists, while others are sycophants who work for their vested interests. And you may find that your boss is not as cordial and approachable as your college professor had been.

To make matters worse, you also encounter a few subordinates who tend to work in a half-hearted manner. Their priorities in life are different. They discuss politics and the country's economy during work hours, enjoy a long afternoon tea, engage in meaningless gossip, and kill their time until you leave the office. And if you would tell them to complete an assignment, they would dillydally, doing no real work and struggling repeatedly to meet project deadlines. Don't get disgruntled by their lackadaisical attitude.

Don't measure them against your values and principles. It doesn't make any sense at all. Things do not work that way in any organization. You need to show a little patience in handling people under you. You have to accept that some employees would be inherently indolent and would proceed at their own pace no matter how much you try pushing them. After all, only 20% of people work actively in any organization, as Italian economist Vilfredo Pareto postulated. You need to be flexible enough not to lose control and express your resentment at the sluggish performance of the remaining 80%.

In a nutshell, flexibility at your workplace is directly linked to your goal of keeping your productivity high, maintaining healthy relations with your colleagues and seniors and, most importantly, preserving your peace of mind. If you're not flexible, very soon you'll end up losing the motivation to work, resulting in what I call 'dislikable dislike' towards your job.

D. FAMILY

Flexibility in your family life is necessary for your professional goals, because what happens in your home is automatically reflected in your work performance. Here is one personal experience to corroborate this proposition.

A few years back, I was having frequent arguments with my wife. As I said earlier, we fought about infinitesimally trivial issues, squandering our precious family time. In retrospect, our arguments seem hilarious as well as worthless. We had conflicting choices regarding dinner, differed on the kind of entertainment program that we wanted to watch on weekends, and our shopping preferences were strikingly dissimilar. We also bickered about our priorities in life. I insisted on spending more time in my profession, while she advised me to give some time to family also. There was a sort of disconnect between our respective aspirations, which stymied my ability to absolutely commit to routine professional assignments at the office. To be absolutely frank with you, at my job, I was present physically but mentally and spiritually, you could have certainly marked me absent.

Though I was familiar with the Buddhist philosophy of choosing the middle path, I lacked the wisdom and the will to apply it in my relationship. I was ignorant of the reality that we must adapt to the needs and priorities of our partner and resort to reconciliation and compromises as and when required, in order to share common domestic space. My obstinate approach wreaked havoc in my personal as well as professional life, until this inflection point.

As I reclined on a chair in my home garden and sipped my favorite Nescafe black coffee as a stimulant before my morning run, I saw something piercingly insightful. Right in front of me, just outside the perimeter of my garden, was a tree that had been completely uprooted due to the fiery thunderstorms the night before. Its branches were broken and lay strewn on the ground in a lifeless state. In contrast to this, there was a small tree nearby that stood erect and firm, with its branches swaying gently back and forth.

Can you guess what worked in this tree's favor?

It was flexibility! All of its structural components—its trunk, branches and leaves—were flexible and strongly interconnected, exerting powerful resistance against air drag. The tree that lay uprooted had met its fatal outcome because it was rigid from top to bottom. As Robert Jordan has articulated it so perfectly, "The oak fought the wind and was broken, the willow bent when it must and survived."

That morning, I learnt that if I had to work on my professional goals peacefully, I had to be flexible like the tree outside my garden, regardless of how turbulent the atmosphere inside my home was. I also realized that a successful married life requires me to have a supple approach towards my partner; it demands a proportionate allocation of time to my work and family. From that moment onwards, my personal life underwent a dramatic transformation and we no longer squabbled about frivolous things.

To conclude this chapter, I have only this to say: you must constantly refine and upgrade your flexibility skills in different fields of life to accomplish your set goals.

Isn't it true that cricketers, soccer players and NBA stars, who frequently travel to different regions to play matches, encounter significant disruptions in their routines and status quo? In this process, they endure drastic changes in food habits, sleep schedules, climate conditions, and their friend circle. Yet, day after day, week after week, and year after year, they deliver exceptional performances in pursuit of their august goals.

You will also be tested and evaluated on similar parameters. For executing peak performance, the everyday environment and conditions will not always be conducive to your whims and fancies, just like it is not for these sportspersons. You will not have your childhood buddies everywhere, you will not get your favorite burger in every town, nor will you get a cozy bedroom at every place or a nice and pleasant atmosphere to work in every time. Only by being flexible and adapting to the circumstances, will you be able to achieve your goals.

Takeaways

- Cultivate flexibility in certain essential aspects of life— food, sleep, work and family—which are critical to accomplishing your goals.

- Flexibility regarding food and sleep is required because you won't always get your favorite food or desired hours of sleep everywhere.

- A flexible work schedule and adaptability at your workplace makes you capable enough to endure all professional challenges.

- Flexibility in your family life is necessary for your professional goals because what happens in your home is often reflected in your work performance.

PENCIL WORK

- Figure out one domain of your life in which you're not flexible and which too often ruins your peace, productivity and relationships.

- Catalogue it in bold letters. And then work towards building flexibility in that domain.

ATOM 3

RESILIENCE

'It is not the strongest of the species that survives, nor the most intelligent, but the one most responsive to change.'

– Charles Darwin

CHAPTER 6

Resilience

'The Third Atom' of the Graphene Mentality

What you will learn in this chapter

- What is resilience?
- What dictates resilience?
- How resilience is necessary to achieve gigantic goals.
- What are three rituals that you need to practice to build resilience?

Some physics. You might not like it, but I need to discuss it before I begin this chapter. And you, too, need to learn it before you proceed further.

So, here is your question: are you familiar with the concept of Young's modulus?

If the answer is on your fingertips, that's terrific. I must complement your memory. But if you don't know, let me explain it. This modulus measures elasticity—the ability of an object to recoil back to its original shape and size when put under stress. The objects which score high on the metric of Young's modulus are more resilient. Researchers have found that the element graphene can withstand a large amount of stretching and bending before fracturing, and thus has staggering resilience. Its Young's modulus is astronomical.

Like the element graphene, when put under severe stress and strain, we should also become resilient enough to regain our original state. If we want to successfully endure all the hardships on the journey to our goals, our physical and psychological resistance to adverse circumstances and unexpected outcomes should be remarkable.

The big question then is, how can we achieve resilience on such a mammoth scale?

Of course, there are certain rituals to do that. But before we elaborate on these rituals, let us first clarify what dictates resilience.

BIG IS NOT BIG AND SMALL IS NOT SMALL

If we take stock of the factors that determine resilience, we easily discern that it is completely an internal game. In the context of humans, it has nothing to do with their physique, personality or behavior. And as far as non-human entities are concerned, it is not linked to their size, structure, shape or external appearance. This is corroborated by the fact that large trees, huge communication towers and gigantic residential complexes, all collapse into rubble in the face of natural disasters like earthquakes, floods or cyclones. At the same time, tiny algae, mussels, nematodes and simple reed houses survive devastation.

The natural corollary which emerges is this: resilience is not proportional to size. Big is not always big. And small is not always small.

Let me illustrate this through a beautiful example.

Considered sui generis, the tardigrade is a tiny water creature famed for its high resilience to extreme weather conditions. It is also known as a water bear. It can endure extreme temperatures and pressures, air deprivation, radiation exposure, dehydration and starvation. Scientists have demonstrated that this eight-legged invertebrate can survive for 30 years without food and water. It can thrive even in a vacuum without oxygen. It is often said that the tardigrade is the only creature that will survive until the Sun dies and will even survive most catastrophic events like an asteroid impact, supernova explosion and gamma ray bursts. About 66 million years ago, when almost three-quarters of the species became extinct due to a possible asteroid impact, the population of tardigrades remained unaffected. The dinosaurs died but the tardigrades survived. This diminutive creature, measuring 1 mm in size, exhibits various mechanisms to withstand harsh conditions.

So, it is irrelevant whether you're small or big in size. You can always take inspiration from this tiny creature and demonstrate resilience to overcome all adversities and challenges on the way to your big goals. Got it?

EXERTING RESILIENCE TO ACHIEVE BIG GOALS

When your goals are enormous, resilience becomes a necessary attribute because such goals can be achieved only if you're willing to undergo gargantuan stress.

Take the example of the small island country, Japan. In 1945, after the Hiroshima and Nagasaki disasters, it suffered huge devastation. In addition to that, recurrent earthquakes in the past also played a big role in debilitating its socio-economic fabric.

Yet, amid these adversities, Japan has successfully achieved its goal of becoming the world's fourth largest economy in terms of nominal GDP. And it boasts of conglomerates like Toyota, Honda, Sony and Hitachi. How could Japan marshal this astounding feat? It is the miracle of their people, for their people. Driven by the strong sense of *ikigai* and trust and catalyzed by their ancient proverbs like *fall seven times, stand up eight,* its citizens are one of the most sincere, honest and diligent people on this planet—a beacon of inspiration for other continents. In unequivocal terms, their prompt responsiveness to the call of national rebuilding after massive disasters has contributed to the success of Japan.

At the age of 36, with 22 Grand Slams under his belt, Rafael Nadal was a ferocious tennis player with a remarkable amount of hunger and passion to win even more. This iconic player had one special quality—the dynamic will to keep persevering despite baffling injuries throughout his career. Analysts had documented that he had suffered almost 31 different kinds of injuries in the past, involving different parts of his body. At one point of time, his career was at the verge of decimation and doctors were highly skeptical of his prospects, advising him to quit tennis. Yet, because of sheer persistence and resilience, he succeeded in playing tennis in an indefatigable manner and conquered all injuries in his pursuit to win more and more accolades.

There is another moment in the history of sports that embodies resilience on a colossal scale. Known as the Miracle of Istanbul, the event I am talking about is the 2005 Champions League final match between Liverpool and AC Milan at Istanbul. AC Milan were the favorites to win and as expected, scored 3 goals in the first half of the match. However, in the second half, Liverpool produced one of the greatest comebacks in the history of soccer and scored 3 goals in quick succession within 6 minutes, to level the score at 3-3. Eventually, Liverpool went on to win the Champions League trophy by defeating AC Milan in penalties.

Nobody knows what transpired in the dressing room during the 15 minutes of halftime. But one thing was obvious. Members of Liverpool Football Club, including the team players, coaching staff, mentors and thousands of fans watching the epic saga from the stands, believed tremendously in pulling off a comeback.

Whether it is Rafael Nadal, Liverpool or the tiny country of Japan, the common element in their success was their inherent strength to exhibit a high Young's modulus during moments of peak stress. When they faced setbacks, their immense resilience and steadfastness ignited their resurgence.

Similarly, if you intend to succeed in your goals, you must showcase supreme resilience to deal with stress as well as setbacks.

BUILDING RESILIENCE TO DEAL WITH STRESS AND SETBACKS

There are three fundamental rituals to help you in this process. The first ritual will help you deal with stress, while the second and third rituals will help you overcome setbacks.

A: BUILDING RESILIENCE TO DEAL WITH STRESS

RITUAL 1: STRESS WEEK

This ritual of Stress Week is a brainchild of the Special Forces, the elite regiments of the Indian Army. They use it quite effectively to test as well as build the quotient of resilience among volunteer candidates. Only those who manifest high tenacity can sustain the immense physical and psychological stress that occurs over a period of one week. The remaining lot suffers mental fractures and surrenders without much resistance, much like egg shells that develop cracks the moment you apply a light pressure.

For building resilience, the usefulness of stress week is evident by the wide array of activities incorporated in the everyday routine highlighted below.

STRESS WEEK
(Daily schedule)

Time	Activity
0500–0600	Running with a 20kg backpack
0600–0630	Swimming Test
0630–0730	Catching fish and frogs
0730–0800	Breakfast
0800- 0900	Written IQ test
0900–1100	Preparation of Hideouts and Trenches
1100–1300	Camouflage, Concealment, Patrolling
1300–1400	Lunch
1400–1500	BOC (Battle obstacle crossing)
1500-1600	Room intervention drill
1600–1730	Game of football
1730–1900	Written IQ test
1900-2000	Dinner
2000–2100	Battle craft, Field craft
2100–2300	Jungle survival drill
2300–0100	Ambush and Raid
0100-0200	Foot march
0200–0500	Sleep

Values tested: resilience, flexibility, team spirit, intelligence, ingenuity

If you have a close look at the range of activities in this schedule, you'll notice that this rigorous routine has been designed in a comprehensive manner with the sole purpose of testing resilience, although it assesses flexibility and team spirit well too. Candidates are subjected to this arduous routine for seven continuous days under the supervision of trained instructors and evaluators who diligently scrutinize their every activity.

The Special Forces include stress week in their evaluation process to ascertain whether candidates are mentally resilient to sustain themselves during actual operations against the enemy, which stretch anywhere from 48 hours to 7 days.

THE SCIENCE OF STRESS WEEK: SPIKES TO PLATEAUS

Practicing the ritual of stress week allows Special Forces combatants to convert cortisol spikes into plateaus—a prerequisite to endure any kind of stress. The fundamental fact is that exposure to stressful activities during the first few days releases an enormous amount of cortisol, the hormone secreted naturally by our body in response to stress. Hence, there is a sudden spike. However, repetition of such activities results in plateauing cortisol levels after mid-week, as the body's physiology gradually adapts to the available stressors.

The only requisite for completing this ritual is that candidates should be patient and courageous enough to not surrender when levels peak during the mid-week mark. Those who complete stress week are indeed the special and extraordinary ones, gifted with the complete gamut of virtues necessary to become a member of

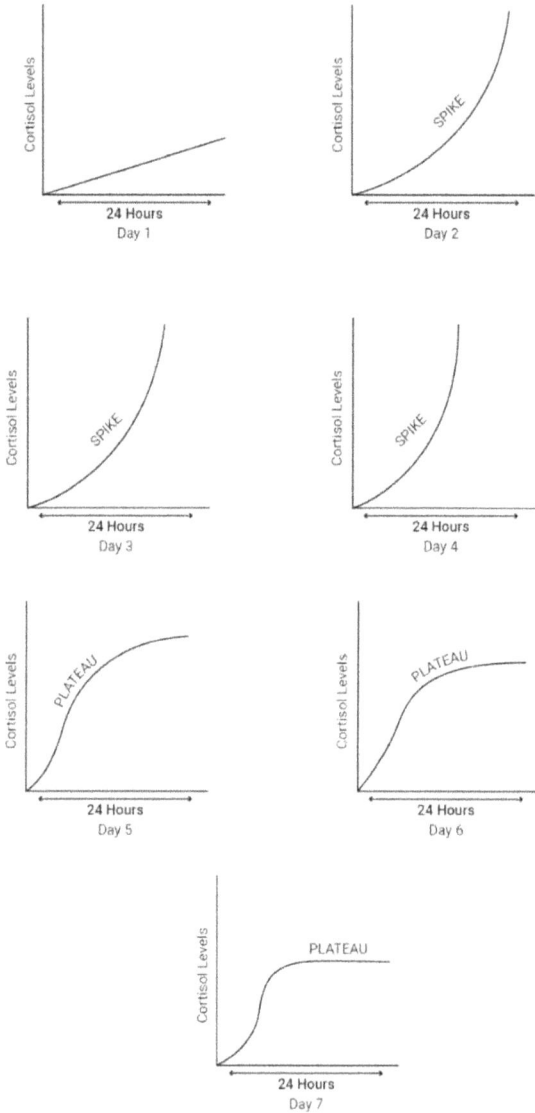

TRANSFORMING CORTISOL SPIKES INTO PLATEAUS THROUGH STRESS WEEK

Special Forces. It is not everyone's forte to score remarkably in the IQ tests despite week-long sleep deprivation and backbreaking all-night foot marches. When lactic acid builds up in the calf muscles and the brain does not receive enough glucose, isn't it marvelous to showcase cognitive prowess and perform brilliantly in IQ tests? That is when the true focus, concentration and attention span of an individual are tested.

You can also become a master of converting spikes into plateaus, but the way to gain mastery is to practice stress week.

HOW SHOULD YOU PRACTICE STRESS WEEK?

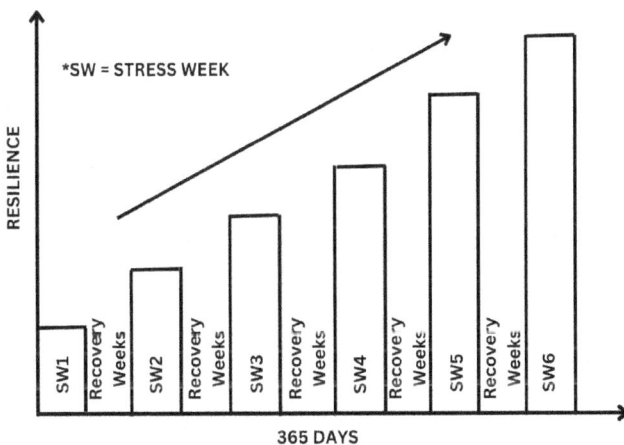

MODEL FOR PRACTISING STRESS WEEKS

Simulate any week as your stress week. Begin your first day by putting yourself under gradual stress. Plan your activities in such a way that you don't get more than five hours of sleep. You don't need to include the strenuous activities that these Special Forces commandos do. Keep your schedule simple, relevant and viable one that is meaningful and constructive for you. You can study literature related to your profession, devote some time to practice your craft, do some creative work like designing a product or formulate concrete plans and strategies to accomplish your goals.

Also, schedule some playtime during the evening or make time for relaxation activities like meditation, yoga or nature walks. Don't eat a heavy dinner because it leads to excessive drowsiness as the blood supply gets diverted from the brain to your gut. You can consume light snacks intermittently if your brain gets foggy and cloudy due to depletion in its glucose levels.

Do this continuously for two days. On the third and fourth days of the stress week, continue with the same activities, but increase stress intensity by reducing your sleep to four hours a day. During the last three days of the week, build more stress in your daily routine and reduce your sleep to just three hours (don't fear, believe me, it's doable). It's okay to feel sleep deprived, confused, disoriented, fatigued and irritated at this stage. But don't quit! Endure it and complete your seven days at any cost. Once done, you'll feel a unique sense of accomplishment and triumph, enough to inseminate this self-belief that you can weather all storms emanating from stressful events in your life.

Keep the next few weeks for recovery before you resume another cycle of stress week. Repeat every two months to complete six stress weeks yearly. Don't practice it every week. Instead of building your resilience, it will break you completely. There is a limit to Young's modulus of elasticity. Even the element graphene has a specific threshold value, and it will break down if you stretch it beyond a certain point. 6 stress weeks in a year need to be complemented by 46 regular weeks to ensure adequate recuperation and recovery. This is the only way to build supreme mental endurance.

If you don't want to do it in isolation, make it a team exercise. Persuade your friends and peers to join you in this amazing feat of resilience. This way, you can instill a sense of competitiveness and collaboration and keep yourself motivated and enthused during the entire process. Team work is a giant fillip to your sovereign spirit.

WHY SHOULD YOU PRACTICE STRESS WEEK?

You might find my recommendation to practice the ritual of stress week contradictory to the benefits of sound sleep and its inherent wonders. But my staunch gospel is that it is of immense practical utility in your life. The efficacy of this unconventional method is also mentioned in one of the *Moral Letters* written by the prodigious Seneca. This is really worth reading not because it endorses my doctrine, but to read the words of one of the most venerated stoic philosophers of all time:

"Here is a lesson to test your mind's mettle: take part of a week in which you have only the most meagre and cheap food, dress scantly in shabby clothes, and ask yourself if this is really the worst that you feared. It is when times are good that you should grind yourself for tougher times ahead, for when Fortune is kind the soul can build defenses against her ravages. So it is that soldiers practice maneuvers in peacetime, erecting bunkers with no enemies in sight and exhausting themselves under no attack so that when it comes, they won't grow tired."

Seneca's message is simple: to secure our fortress of endurance and doggedness, we should purposefully forego our possessions, privileges and luxuries and, once in a while, expose ourselves to an oppressive environment. To strengthen our tolerance and sturdiness, we should deliberately remove our persona and patina and expose our core character to the assault of poverty and pauperism. That's what we get to do when we complete the foundational course of stress week.

Pick up your pencil and write my words on your personal parchment: after undergoing self-engineered pain, the practical gains are phenomenal. Subjecting yourself to harshness and toughness through stress weeks yields many benefits. First of all, it helps you deal with sleep disruptions. We know that we can't be fortunate enough to get the 7-8 hours of healthy sleep required for optimum brain function every day. As we discussed in the chapter on flexibility, we must always be prepared to endure sleep disruptions. Because the following morning everyone will expect a splendid performance from us, despite uneven sleep at night. And we can't deliver a magical performance without practicing the ritual of stress weeks, which will accustom us to such inadvertent disruptions.

One more reason why you should practice mock stress weeks. It helps a lot when you face the actual stress week of your life, where you need to prepare and perform quickly without succumbing to pressure. It makes you resilient to acute stress that arises while working on any goal that needs to be executed in a very short span of time. To understand this better, let us consider those people around us who work in an extremely pressing environment with a limited time window to complete their grand projects.

Every year, a week before their thesis presentation, thousands of PhD scholars go into hyper-diligent mode and spend sleepless nights studying the literature relevant to their dissertation. Across the globe, a week before semester exams, tens of thousands of students start burning the midnight oil to revise the entire syllabus at rocket speed. A week before the unveiling of their product or service, several CEOs hold brainstorming and troubleshooting sessions with key stakeholders to eliminate any fiasco at the last moment. Similarly, a week before the launch date of their flagship project, many space scientists start pulling all-nighters and thoroughly go through the standard operating procedures, checking all the minute details.

Do you think that everyone succeeds in delivering at the crunch moment? Absolutely not! Only those students, scholars, CEOs and scientists survive the rigors of acute stress who have pushed themselves during sessions and sessions of mock stress weeks in the past. Countless students fail to crack their semester exams, numerous scholars perform miserably during their thesis presentation, plenty of CEOs are left ruing after a disastrous launch of their product, and many scientists get dejected after launch failures.

The crux of the matter is that whatever your profession, exposing yourself to an adequate number of mock stress weeks enables you to supplement your reserves of resilience and strength required to face the real stress week. As the old maxim goes, "the more you sweat in peace, the less you bleed in war."

B: BUILDING RESILIENCE TO OVERCOME SETBACKS

RITUAL 2: GPS

There are going to be multiple occasions in life when you will face horrifying setbacks and your goals will seem unattainable. Even after you combine your passion with your intrinsic acumen, there is no guarantee that you will be immune from shocking results you don't expect. Setbacks can be really painful, with debilitating wounds and aches that take a considerable amount to recuperate fully.

The second ritual of GPS is a time-tested method for quick recovery after such traumatic setbacks.

The Daily Ritual of GPS to Build Resilience

GPS stands for gratitude, psychosocial support system, and self-belief.

G: Gratitude

All of us practice gratitude in subtle as well as obvious ways. We have internalized this habit because of our parents and teachers. When I was in boarding school, we followed this wonderful ritual after finishing our meals. We thanked the Almighty through the prayer, "Thank you, God, for what I have received. Amen!" It was such a powerful way of expressing gratitude. I have personally incorporated this prayer in my life, and whenever something special and joyful happens to me, I always express my gratitude through it.

For instance, I did this when I received my first salary, when I purchased my first vehicle, when I constructed my new home (with my hard-earned savings and investments), when I brought home my pet when he was just 30 days old, and when my son was born. Acknowledging our gratitude to God makes us humble and ensures that our accomplishments do not get to our heads.

Gratitude benefits us a lot!

However, most of us practice gratitude only when the outcomes are in our favor. We are extremely reluctant to express gratitude in the face of tragic reversals and blows. We don't thank God or anyone else when we fail, have a breakup, or lose a near and dear one. Let me narrate to you the story of a brave lady whose life aptly teaches us how and why we must practice gratitude when we meet with unfortunate events in our life.

She is a living legend. Her name is Helen Keller. Though she was born a healthy child on June 27, 1880, in Tuscumbia, Alabama, when she was just nineteen months old, an unknown illness made her completely blind and deaf. Despite this major tragedy, she didn't give up on learning to read and write like an average person. The transformative moment in her life came when she met Anne Sullivan, her teacher, who was also blind. Anne taught her all the words through hand spelling. She learnt her first word, 'doll', when Anne brought one for her and put it in one of her hands and simultaneously spelled out 'd-o-l-l' on the palm of the other hand. Thus, by connecting objects with letters, she learned thousands of words.

With perseverance and courage, she became a writer and published her autobiography, *The Story of My Life* in 1903. A person who could not see nor hear went on to write a book. A heroic feat indeed! Through her written words, she communicated with the external world and travelled across the globe, giving lectures on different topics. She also consistently advocated for the rights of blind people and her efforts culminated in the establishment of rehabilitation centers for them across the United States.

She could pull off such valiant deeds because, every day before going to bed, she practiced gratitude. Take a quick peek at some of her impactful quotes.

"When one door of happiness closes, another opens, but often we look so long at the closed door that we do not see the one which has been opened for us."

"I thank God for my handicaps for, through them, I have found myself, my work, and my God."

"So much has been given to me I have no time to ponder over that which has been denied."

Expressing gratitude is a fabulous way to build the resilience required to overcome setbacks in life.

You can also practice gratitude in another form. You can use negative visualization. In this technique, you imagine that you're not the only person who has failed; millions of others are equally devastated and there will be thousands among these millions who have failed more miserably than you. Negative visualization is a useful habit to let go of feelings of despondency and somberness. And there cannot be a better way of practicing it than remembering another memorable quote by Hellen Keller, "I cried because I had no shoes until I met a person who had no feet."

P: Psychosocial support system

After a major setback, it is pretty common to find plenty of people who are liberal in offering us 2 Cs (criticism and consolation). But how effective are these 2 Cs in rebuilding out of the rubble? Not much, in my opinion. Reconstructing our house of dreams from the wreckage of our failures requires a third C, more colossal in size and proportion than the other two. Courage! But regrettably, there is an acute shortage of people around us willing to lend this necessary third C.

Strive to build an everlasting ecosystem of close friends who are optimistic and keen to inject courage every time you fall into the abyss of sadness. Search for appropriate mentors who can teach you a step-wise methodological approach to get out of the morass. They're the ones who should be your 'anytime look-up-to' club members, whom you'd approach straightway during hardships instead of faith-healers and phony therapists. Their mental reinforcement will instill in you fresh enthusiasm to rise again. These rare motivators, who can inject you with the third C, play a significant role in resurrecting your killer instincts. They are your real supporters, while the 2 Cs peddlers are fake.

S: Self-belief

"One person with a belief is equal to ninety-nine who have only interests," noted the erudite John Stuart Mill. Cultivating the habit of self-belief in the event of failure is of paramount significance. It is the only proven strategy to regain the will and confidence required to resume battle. Don't feel shattered and resign yourself to your fate, whether you fail in competitive exams, your private venture goes into ruins, or your hopes of winning accolades in sports are threatened because of some severe injury. Despite fatal misfortunes in the past, believe in yourself that you can still crack any exam, that you can always revive your collapsed start-up, and that you can yet win medals and earn laurels in your game.

Take a strategic break for a few days after any big failure. Rest, recoup and start recapitulating these positive phrases in your mind:

I can rise from the ashes like the phoenix did.

I have all the wherewithal to bounce back after failures.

I'm gutsy enough to reproduce winning knocks that I did so often in the past.

There is still plenty of oomph and zeal left within me.

Repeat these phrases to yourself to remind your mind of its immense capability to begin again from scratch.

GPS is an incredibly efficacious ritual to bounce back after a disastrous event. Let's validate its visceral power through a tale of pure grit and determination.

The story is about Commander Sanjeev Khatri, a naval officer and one of my classmates, who deployed GPS to crack the SSB. SSB or Services Selection Board is a rare and unique system of evaluation devised to select candidates who have the potential to become defense officers. It is a mandatory process before you can join the defense forces. All volunteers who get fascinated by the "Do you have it in you?" posters on highways must traverse this arduous road to prove whether they have it in them or not.

Spanning five days, it is an elaborate appraisal system comprising various tests like PPDT (Picture Perception and Description Test), WAT (Word Association Test), Group Discussion, and Psychology Assessment. It scans you thoroughly, from top to bottom, and diagnoses whether you have OLQs (Officer-Like Qualities) such as initiative, ingenuity and a positive mindset. People usually say that it is relatively easy to crack the IIT or CAT exam, but it is extremely difficult to clear SSB. That it is a rigorous process is vindicated by this fact—Amitabh Bachchan, Shah Rukh Khan, and Dr APJ Abdul Kalam, and many others who are splendid achievers in their fields, have taken the SSB, but they couldn't make it.

However, if your ardor and passion are sublime, and the will to undergo this excruciating ordeal is supreme, then no one can stop you from cracking SSB.

Sanjeev cleared SSB in his eighteenth attempt. Isn't it incredible? Would you believe he had enough patience to stick till the eighteenth try? Whenever I recall what he went through during all those attempts, it buttresses my belief that you can't attain hero status without showing resilience and tenacity. I remember the first time he failed—he returned home devastated that he hadn't made it to the exceptional league of Army officers. But that did not stop him from introspecting about what went wrong, and coming up with a plan to rectify the mistakes and improve in his next attempt.

He persevered again after getting over the brief period of dejection and practiced honing his communication skills in front of a mirror by speaking on a diverse range of topics. He was very confident during the second attempt and was highly optimistic about his prospects because of the sheer hard work he had put in. Yet, for reasons not discernible, he was again rejected and returned disheartened. This process repeated for seventeen consecutive attempts like a Sisyphean loop. On each occasion, when he failed, he experienced a fresh spike of self-doubt, hatred, fear and defeatism, making it an uphill task to restart every time.

However, he invoked the GPS ritual to negotiate all this negativity.

After every failure, he would express gratitude for what he had learnt, was consoled and encouraged by trustworthy members of his psychosocial support system and mustered the necessary self-belief and spunk to not relinquish his ambition. After getting knocked down seventeen times, he rose again, and showed his audacity in facing the crucible for the last time. Finally, in his eighteenth attempt, he cracked SSB!

GPS is effective not only for getting through SSB. You can use it to navigate your way to success in every fiefdom that you intend to conquer.

RITUAL 3: LGF

The Daily Ritual of LGF to Build Resilience

The ritual of LGF, or Live-Give-Forgive, is another time-tested method for your steady recovery after heartbreaking setbacks.

When we're in deep dejection and agony after misfortunes, we choose different strategies to palliate our aching heart and relieve our choked-up throat. We vent our pent-up emotions, seek psychotherapies such as CBT and Morata, or employ various ego-defense mechanisms (projection, rationalization, sublimation, etc.) to suppress our feelings and distract our mind. At the most, we resign ourselves to our fate, acknowledge and accept the painful reality, and gradually move out of grief, as Kübler-Ross prescribed in her five stages approach to mitigate any grief.

All this is such complicated stuff. Or should I say, esoteric?

I'm offering you a more practical and simpler version: LGF, an easy acronym to remember and practice, without any need to book a session with bogus faith healers who will sell you their own concoctions, promising instant Nirvana.

LGF: Live, Give and Forgive

I used this ritual of Live-Give-Forgive when I suffered the first major setback of my life. And I can say with immense conviction that it definitely helps you to move past harrowing moments. The setback I am talking about occurred in 2004. I failed in clearing the entrance examination to Armed Forces Medical College (AFMC)—a prestigious institute that select just 150 of the nation's brightest minds each year. It was devastating because I did not expect this shocking result. I had been confident that I would pass the exam and had prepared thoroughly, with hundreds of mock tests where I had done well and scored excellent marks.

The neighbors in my village mocked me. I could hear their taunts—"Why did he go to boarding school if he had to come back here jobless? Why did he waste his father's money?" My father was irked at my performance, too. He rebuked me for squandering my time and predicted that I would not get any job in life if I continued like this. It led to serious arguments between us, resulting in a verbal duel where he counted on his fingers the reasons for my failure. In retaliation, I kept on justifying my poor result, blaming it on luck, lack of guidance and fierce competition, though none of these factors were culpable.

The next day, I packed my books and clothes in a duffle bag and without telling my mother, left home with this pledge: I will not return until I crack this examination. Along with two other classmates who were also preparing for the same exam, I rented a 10x10 ft room in a city located 25 km from my village. The three of us stayed in that tiny room. I shouldn't even call it a room. It was more like a corporate employee's cubicle. We had to move the bed out and sleep on mattresses on the ground to create some space for us to move around. It also had a tiny attached bathroom-cum-toilet in one corner.

It had been a week since I had left my home, but my mind still struggled to process my father's harsh words and the disparaging jibes of my neighbors. I could not concentrate on my studies. And as my exam date came closer, this took a huge mental toll. My mind could not think clearly. I had to find some way out of this scary fogginess. It was then that I decided to embrace the ritual of 'live, give and forgive' for complete recovery.

I chose to *live my life* in a way that would make me happy. I laughed with my roommates. We recounted the pranks we had done together at school and wished for a time machine to take us back to 1997. We contributed money and bought some gym equipment for evening workouts so that we could build up muscle and capture the attention of girls at our coaching center. We watched movies, played cards, shared anecdotes and enjoyed every moment. I lived to relax my mind; I lived to enrich my soul; I lived to be at peace with myself; and I lived for inner joy.

I *gave myself time* for complete recovery. I gave time to my friends to make them equal partners in my healing process, and I gave happiness to the people around me. When I lived in the company of my close friends, I realized that there was no point in feeling guilty after failures. I ought to love myself when there was so much abundance in my life… with no poverty of any kind.

I *forgave myself* by annihilating the guilt, self-hatred and scarcity—feelings that had been transplanted from outside into my psyche. And when I succeeded in forgiving myself, I could forgive my father for his blunt words and my neighbors for their derisive remarks. I forgot everything.

Self-forgiveness is a stepping stone to forgiving others. Unfortunately, most people do the opposite. They try to forgive others without forgiving themselves, and ultimately end up struggling with the relics of a grudge, anger and acrimony resurfacing in intermittent spurts. Just as you learn to write alphabets before words and to say Dad before Grandpa and to play chords before a song, you need to forgive yourself first before you can think of forgiving others. The former is a *sine qua non* for the latter.

To sum up, it was this LGF principle that helped me detoxify completely. It acted as an illuminating lamp, which showed me the way out of darkness and conferred strength within me, to fight back for my goal. I regained my flow to study with better focus and intensity and cleared the exam in the next attempt.

When it comes to coping strategies after failures, GPS is an immediate savior. However, the ritual of LGF provides long-term, sustainable relief. Practice it in the face of any agonizing setback in your goal journey and, believe me, it will provide you the necessary impetus to move on as early as possible.

Essential tips to perform this ritual are highlighted through this triangle:

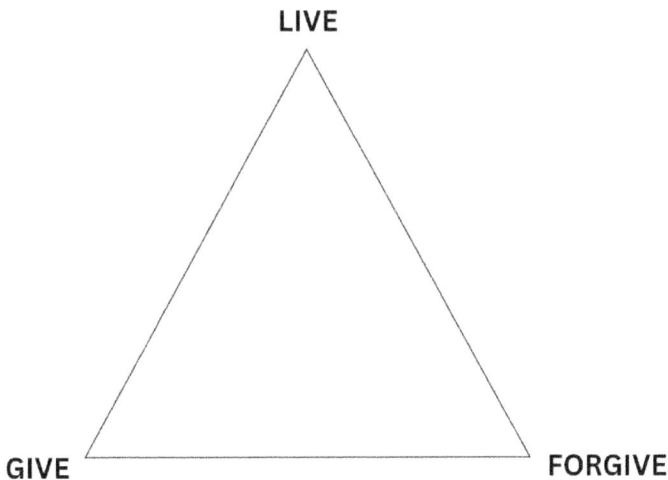

LIVE

GIVE   FORGIVE

RITUAL OF LGF

Live

Live your life the way you want to live.

Do thrilling and adventurous activities to beat the emptiness.

Spend time with your near and dear ones for peace and solace.

Give

Give smiles and happiness to people around you to remain happy.

Give help to others. Your soul is purified when you see the positive difference you make in their lives.

Give knowledge to others. It amplifies your worth when you see their intellectual growth happening because of you. This is especially effective after failures when you feel worthless and tend to curse your existence.

Give yourself time for healing. Life automatically becomes okay after some time.

Forgive

Forgive yourself for your mistakes to get rid of guilt and remorse.

Forgive others for their betrayal, cheating and lies to eliminate anger and resentment.

Takeaways

- Resilience is the psychological resistance to endure stress and setbacks in life.

- Resilience is necessary to achieve big goals because stress and setbacks are inevitable parts of your goal journey.

- To deal with stress, embrace the concept of stress week followed by the Special Forces. Practice at least six mock stress weeks yearly to prepare yourself for the actual stress week.

- To overcome setbacks, practice the rituals of GPS and LGF.

PENCIL WORK

- Take out your calendar and mark the weeks that you will practice as stress weeks. This labelling is important for, as you know, intentions incite actions.

- Recall the last time you failed abjectly in any of your missions. Did you blame people, luck, the system or circumstances for your setbacks? Tick YES or NO.

- If yes, then take a firm resolution (in fact, make an inscription) that you won't repeat such a futile exercise ever again in your life. Instead, write down the two fabulous acronyms that you have just learnt. And promise yourself that you will deploy them to engineer your resurgence every time you face a setback.

STEP 4: **COOPERATE**

ATOM 4

TEAM SPIRIT

'There is no such thing as a self-made man. You will reach your goals only with the help of others.'

– George Shinn

CHAPTER 7

Team Spirit

'The Fourth Atom' of the Graphene Mentality

Whtat you will learn in this chapter

- How team spirit is critical to achieve your personal as well as collective goals.
- What is the twin MAT system for cultivating team spirit in your respective sphere?
- How you can use the TAD trident to achieve your team goals.

Please have a look at the element graphene.

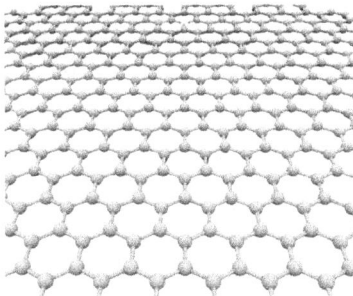

ELEMENT **GRAPHENE**

If you analyze its structure closely, you'll notice that each carbon atom is intimately linked to three other carbon atoms, making a honeycomb lattice. This unique arrangement, displaying tremendous team effort between every atom, accounts for the high elasticity and resilience of this element. If a carbon atom does not hold the hand of its nearest neighbor, the entire structure of graphene will collapse immediately. This symbolizes that without team spirit, a foundation remains fragile. It is the atom of team spirit that delivers strength and resilience to any structure, system or organization.

Observe any inanimate object around you: a chair, table, fan, a bed, or any structure like a wall, ceiling or the floor. Externally, each one of these looks like a composite and complete entity, but internally, at a microscopic level, there are many elements and molecules which coalesce together to give it a definite form and shape. Without this intrinsic support, these objects and structures would simply cease to exist. Even a single brick which joins with another brick, and so on, to make a huge monument, will crumble if its ingredients like silica, clay and lime do not cooperate with each other.

For that matter, analyze your own body structure. It is not made up of just muscles and bones; it is a smorgasbord of thousands of cells that merge to become tissues, which further inter-connect to form organs—the liver, kidney, heart and lungs. If, at an organic level, these biological units and sub-units do not work together, you would be dead in no time. In other words, if all the atomic components of your body do not display team spirit, your body will turn into dust and ashes. Team spirit is the basis for existence and survival of all, whether it is a non-living thing or a living being.

Now you must be wondering, how is this atom of team spirit relevant to the process of achieving our goals?

Well, you can embark on your goals with firmness, endure all challenges with flexibility and resilience, but in your journey towards success, you will definitely need the attribute of team spirit at some point. As individuals, we have plenty of constraints—our cranial capacity is just 1200 cc, there is a finite limit to which we can process challenges and work pressures, our emotions fluctuate hourly, our mood oscillates daily, and we don't have an animated will and intent all the time.

The other factor is that there are always certain activities that our colleagues can do better than us, and it is wise to delegate such things to them so that we can prioritize the work we are good at doing. Smart people don't follow the herd mentality, but they are brilliant at working with the herd. "I can do things you cannot, you can do things I cannot; together we can do great things"—the magnanimous Catholic nun Mother Teresa's words synopsize it so beautifully.

Winning is not an individual game, it's a team game. It's not a solitary battle, it's a collective war. You need to cooperate with your colleagues, for it is the most efficient and economical way of winning and an effortless and speedy way to reach your destination. A detailed analysis of the sterling record of Jonas Vingegaard, the two-time Tour de France winner, attests my proposition.

The Tour de France is an annual cycling championship and is considered the ultimate crucible of endurance and stamina in the sporting world. Cyclists cover a total distance of 3,630 km, and ride continuously over 21 days, competing fiercely for the coveted yellow jersey awarded to the rider leading general classification. The race consists of 21 stages, conducted across different terrains—flats, mountains and cobblestones, all extremely grueling rides. Danish cyclist Vingegaard won the Tour de France in 2022 and 2023, beating Slovenian Tadej Pogačar in a closely contested race.

But here is the caveat: Vingegaard's triumph is not just a tale of individual grit and determination; it actually portrays uncanny team spirit and remarkable cooperation among all eight riders on his team. Though he is the most prodigious rider of the Jumbo-Visma team, he is constantly supported on the tour circuit by other riders who are popularly called "domestiques." Their primary role is to shield him from deadly crashes in the peloton, act as pacers in the mountains, provide him energy drinks for recovery, and even replace his cycle if it gets punctured or damaged.

Vingegaard succeeded in winning two titles not only due to his cycling talent and skills but also because of the selfless loyalty and support from these domestiques. Unambiguously, he was firm in his belief to achieve his personal goal, had enough flexibility to adapt to ride on diverse terrains, and certainly, was considerably resilient while enduring stressful and competitive environments. Yet, had his team members not collaborated, it would have been almost impossible for him to clinch his victories. Not only Vingegaard but elite athletes across all sports have a core team of different specialists working for them 24x7, engaged in fine tuning their diet, physiotherapy, mental conditioning and mentoring.

Sports is one arena. Achievers in other fields like scientists, artists and business tycoons also need the assistance of behind-the-curtain workers who can contribute in one form or another to make them champions.

Team spirit thus provides the much-needed impetus to achieve our personal goals. At the same time, it is also essential for us to achieve our collective goals because it empowers us to withstand challenges that are common to us all. Consider our fight against Covid-19. We witnessed its horrific effects—the tough lockdowns, countless deaths, surging unemployment and poverty, the nation's plummeting economy.

However, we fought this pandemic as a team and engineered collective solutions to overcome its challenges. Various entrepreneurs marshaled their capital and ingenuity to manufacture tons of sanitizers, spraying machines, masks, face shields and PPE kits. And when resources were overwhelmed, our Covid warriors—police personnel, doctors, nurses, paramedical staff and housekeepers—worked relentlessly to mitigate the loss and damage. The team spirit of all these heroes imparted the necessary resilience we needed to stay afloat and helped us achieve the astonishing goal of vaccinating our entire population.

Team effort is more potent than individual brilliance. Eleven mediocre people operating in an interdependent manner are always better than one genius working independently and alone. Take the example of the Portuguese football team. Everyone knows that Cristiano Ronaldo is a footballing genius. Yet, Portugal has not won too many prominent tournaments on the international stage and has sometimes suffered ignominious defeats against average teams. It is the team effort that counts, not the chutzpah of a single person.

Look at any colossal company—Apple, Amazon, Google, Facebook. They have been successful not because of the individual effort of a dynamic CEO, a meticulous CFO, or a smart and charismatic marketing head. They are flourishing because of the commitment of every employee working in different sectors—customer satisfaction, grievance redressal, design and development, sales, marketing and finance. Their collective effort imparts strength and resilience to these firms to survive in times of financial crisis and market failures.

If team spirit is such a game changer, then how can we cultivate team spirit to accomplish our collective goals?

CULTIVATING TEAM SPIRIT THROUGH 'TWIN MATS'

To cultivate team spirit, you can employ twin MATs (MAT 1 and MAT 2). I have handcrafted them especially for you with fine threads and the exquisite embroidery of my life teachings.

First, let us deconstruct MAT 1.

MAT 1: MINDSET, APPROACH, TOLERANCE

Mindset

A long time ago, my friend Gurdeep and I set out on an adventurous trip to the majestic Himalayas, to capture their picturesque landscape strewn with diverse flora and fauna. After a day-long exhausting trek, we decided to relax outdoors. The night was serene, lit by a silvery moon, and innumerable stars scattered across the sky like city lights.

As my friend photographed the mesmerizing peaks and breathtaking landscape with his DSLR camera, I asked him, "Buddy, which do you like the most—mountains, islands, deserts or beaches?"

"Islands, of course!" he was quick in his response. He then could not resist recollecting his last summer trip to the sinking island of Venice, where he had enjoyed fascinating gondola rides along the Grand Canal.

After he finished sharing his trip memories, I interjected again, "Gurdeep, don't you think that mountains and islands are radically different?"

"How?" he enquired.

"Different response to similar conditions," I replied. "See, though both mountains and islands are subjected to the tectonic forces of nature, one is gradually rising—geologists have proven that the average height of mountains increases at the rate of 0.5 cm per year due to tectonic forces—while the other is slowly sinking."

"Sounds interesting! I had no clue about that," he admitted, clearly intrigued. "But why this different effect when the cause is same? When the process is common, the outcome should be similar. Every action should have an equal and opposite reaction." He invited me to explain the science behind it.

"Here is the thing," I said, "mountains rise because their peaks are interconnected and show extreme cooperation when enduring earthquakes, landslides and avalanches. Despite these natural catastrophes and constant wear and tear, mountains are determined to rise steadily every single day. In contrast, islands are sinking because they're scattered and separated from each other, and can't cooperate to confront natural challenges such as tsunamis, cyclones, glacial melts and the consequent rise in water levels. And when exposed to stress, their response is largely reactionary and manifests as lava effusing from the huge magma chambers underneath."

He chuckled. "I feel this is more your philosophical perspective rather than scientific insight." I wished I could have told him that science and philosophy are two sides of the same coin, reinforcing each other in a significant way. After all, epic philosophers like Aristotle and Kant made significant scientific contributions, just as scientists like Galileo, Einstein, Newton and Niels Bohr relied on abstract thoughts while solving the intricate complexities of the universe.

But rather than getting into a debate, I conceded.

"You may be right," I said, leaning in. "I just want to convey that mountains and islands are not only geographical features, they are also strong metaphors for two kinds of mindsets—the Mountain Mindset and the Island Mindset. The kind of mindset we follow directly impacts our lives."

Bemused, Gurdeep raised an eyebrow—a signal for me to explain the differences between the two mindsets before we retreated to our den for the night.

This sketch depicts the gist of the differences.

Mountain Mindset	Vs	Island Mindset
• Rising		• Sinking
• Cooperative		• Secluded
• Creative		• Reactionary
• Resilient		• Vulnerable

You should also exhibit a mountain mindset and strive for cooperation and collaboration with others, just like mountains strive to increase their height under the impact of tectonic forces. Your mindset is the only rare resource that you can neither inherit nor extract through deep-sea mining. It can only be nurtured through conscious and relentless endeavors.

Approach

On the second day of our trip, as we resumed our trek, a beehive swarming with humming bees captured our attention, forcing us to temporarily halt. But since it did not trouble us much, we soon continued ahead. Later, when I returned to my den, I realized that nature is such a great repository of profound lessons.

A beehive is one of the greatest examples of division of labor and team effort. Within a beehive, there are three types of bees operating in a harmonious and synergistic manner to execute their respective roles. The queen bee is responsible for laying eggs, the drones are entrusted with the task of mating, and the worker bees are responsible for fetching food, protecting the hive from intruders and taking care of the queen. Another fantastic fact about worker bees is that they are terrific communicators, conveying information about food availability in the vicinity through a waggle dance.

The flawless teamwork of all the three different kind of bees yields the sumptuous product called honey, which is packaged, distributed and sold globally, ultimately reaching billions of dining tables. And while people relish the taste of honey by adding it to their lemon water or green tea, they seldom are curious about the beehive itself—the site of its production. Here we get one of the most powerful techniques for effective work management, the Honeybee Approach.

I have personal experience to share that highlights how this approach is radically important when you're working in a team.

After completing my graduation in 2010, while I was doing my internship in the emergency department of Military Hospital, Pathankot, I received a patient with a severe head injury. His condition was critical and the Glasgow Coma Scale was 5/15 (a scoring system used to assess the level of consciousness), an extremely low score indicating poor prognosis. Immediately, I called the surgeon on duty and after speaking to him, took the patient to the CT scan center for brain imaging. The radiologist confirmed a 1.5cm x 1.5cm hematoma (blood clot) in the left hemisphere of the brain. It had to be operated on urgently because it was compressing other vital regions in his brain, which could cease his normal respiration and heart activity. So, I promptly moved him to the Operation Theatre, where a team comprising a surgeon, an anesthetist, a nurse and few paramedics, was ready with all the required surgical equipment.

The patient was put under general anesthesia before the surgeon began the operation by making an incision on his scalp. He created a hole in his skull with a drill, removed the bone flap to gain access to the hematoma and evacuated it successfully. This procedure is called burr-hole craniotomy. The bone flap was replaced, and the surgery was over. It took almost two hours for the entire procedure but we achieved our goal of saving the patient's life.

Had we not used the honeybee approach for division of labor, it would have been impossible to salvage his life. The radiologist diagnosed the hematoma, the anesthetist induced anesthesia, the surgeon did the craniotomy, and the nurse, paramedics and

I assisted in the surgery. Each of us played our respective roles in our common objective to save the patient's life.

Tolerance

I learnt the significance of this last component of MAT during my recent trip to Kerala. As I sat on Kovalam beach facing the Arabian Sea and watching the tides ebb and flow in cycles, I could not help but mull over this: the sea is the only entity which allows all objects to merge into it without any prejudice, making it the true embodiment of inclusivity. The sea never discriminates between rivers based on their origin, flow, color or contents. Whether a stream is pure and crystal clear, or it is contaminated and murky, and whether it originates from the state of Maharashtra or Karnataka, the sea treats all of them with equal kindness.

Not only this, the sea is also impartial when providing shelter and food to all species that seek refuge in its vast territory, from tiny planktons to turtles, crustaceans and gigantic dolphins. It also allows people of all categories to traverse through it, be it traders, explorers, tourists, rescue personnel, or even pirates and terrorists. You can also fathom its power of tolerance from the way it endures colossal atrocities such as oil spills, plastic dumping, resource extraction and rampant fishing. Despite this surfeit of mayhem, it does not show any resentment or extract revenge.

You must imbibe this value of tolerance from one of the biggest ecosystems in this world. Just as the sea does not discriminate between rivers, you, too, should not discriminate among people based on their color, region, language, beliefs and opinions. And if you are hurt by someone's unexpected behavior or verbal abuse or blatant critique, maintain a calm and placid attitude like the sea.

Absorb everything even if you disagree. Don't react immediately. Let your heightened emotions die down. And soak like a sponge, no matter how dirty and repugnant is the ink they're throwing at you. As writer Evelyn Beatrice Hall writes in *The Friends of Voltaire*, "I disapprove of what you say, but I will defend to the death your right to say it."

Along with a mountain mindset and a honeybee approach, your sea-like tolerance will make a perfect recipe for a complete team person. By incorporating MAT in your life, you will make your thought process more progressive, intentions less self-centered, and seek companionship over one-upmanship. MAT not only helps make you a team player but also stokes the overall team spirit of your organization. If all your colleagues are willing to work in MAT mode, there will be no friction, no unhealthy competition, and it will be smooth sailing towards a common goal.

FLY LIKE A PELICAN AND SWIM LIKE A TURTLE

Have you ever wondered how migratory birds like pelicans travel every year from one continent to another in pursuit of their foraging missions?

Is it due to their lone-wolf perseverance and stubbornness?

Not at all.

It is because of their team effort!

In 2001, Henri Weimerskirch, a French marine ornithologist, did some interesting research. He attached tiny monitoring devices to the backs of great white pelicans and measured their wing-beat frequency and heart rate as they flew in a V formation. He observed that the frequency of wing movements and their heart rate was lower when they flew in this formation, as compared to their solo flights. That is, they saved almost 11-14% energy flying together. Flying in a V formation allows every bird to lift itself by utilizing the upward flow of air created by the bird in front of it. And when the leading bird gets tired, it drops back to the tail and the rear ones takes its position. Every member of the flock is cooperative and demonstrates a mountain mindset while flying in this formation.

Besides that, they also use the honeybee approach to divide key roles among themselves, such as sensing dangers, alerting other members by honking, and taking care of the injured in case anyone falls sick. During their journey, they display a staggering tolerance to natural hazards like tornados, heavy rains and predators. Working as a team, they endure air resistance and make aerodynamics conducive to their flight, which empowers them to fly seamlessly until they reach their destination. MAT helps them to achieve their collective goal.

In addition to pelicans, there is another creature that employs MAT for a similar purpose. It is the Olive Ridley turtle. Every year, for mass nesting, millions of female turtles swim thousands of miles to reach Gahirmatha—a coastal area in the state of Odisha. En route, they also face sea predators and adverse events like cyclones and strong ocean currents. Yet, swimming with the mountain mindset and tremendous tolerance, they successfully arrive at the beach to lay eggs, which hatch into baby turtles that soon make their first trek towards the ocean. This is the power of team spirit. Events like tsunamis can swallow gigantic whales and dolphins, but not the Olive Ridley turtles.

If you want your team to overcome any obstacle you encounter on the way to your collective goals, you should also fly like a pelican and swim like a turtle.

After dissecting MAT 1, let us decrypt MAT 2 and its role in building team spirit.

MAT 2: MUTUAL ASSESSMENT TOOL

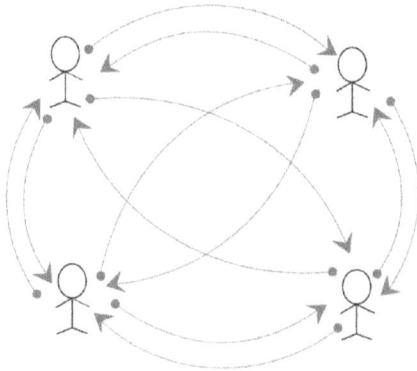

VALUES ASSESSED
- Integrity
- Sincerity
- Humility
- Initiative
- Team Spirit

MUTUAL ASSESSMENT TOOL

Like stress week, the mutual assessment tool is also a brainchild of the Special Forces. Just as the peer review process is crucial for publishing deserving articles in reputed journals, the mutual assessment tool is necessary for selecting worthy candidates for the Special Forces.

It is a unique system in which it is mandatory for every candidate to evaluate their colleagues on certain well-defined yardsticks, one of which is team spirit. This tool is incorporated in the probation curriculum because Special Forces want team players and not individual achievers. Officers are usually organized into small teams which are more swift, lethal and efficient in executing Special Operations.

Can we replicate and implement this model universally?

We must. All institutes with a natural predilection for performance evaluation through an annual or quarterly appraisal by the boss, need to internalize MAT and rejig their existing landscape. Because in the antiquated evaluation system where the boss takes the call, the deep-rooted malaise is that it encourages pernicious trends like sycophancy and kowtowing to the seniors. It rewards trumpet blowers more than the silent performers. Besides, this traditional method of evaluation, though it determines values like accountability and efficiency in a reasonably good manner, fails to capture other attributes like selflessness and synergy required while working in a group.

Don't you agree that we need to desist from such obsolete methods and evolve our appraisal apparatus?

There is a pressing need to incorporate feedback from colleagues and clients when assessing every employee. Unfortunately, very few companies or organizations are undertaking such a holistic and comprehensive scan of their employees. There are only a few outliers, like Google. This renowned tech firm believes in peer review and 360-degree feedback, on a pattern similar to MAT, while hiring employees as well as during their annual performance evaluation.

MAT 2 is indeed a prolific, cost-effective intervention with massive dividends in the long term. In their quest to score better on mutual assessment ranking, employees tend to be more cooperative and less selfish. Instead of competing against each other, they look forward to complementing each other, eventually amplifying the system's overall efficiency. MAT 2 has unfettered potential to spawn a new generation of team warriors who can work for collective goals and not merely individual careers. This is much desired in the present era where the obligation to serve an organization is more critical than a personal commitment to accumulate name, fame and wealth.

TAD TRIDENT:
A WEAPON TO CONQUER YOUR TEAM GOALS

MAT 1 and MAT 2 are effective tools to cultivate team spirit, but the weapon that empowers you to conquer team goals is the TAD Trident.

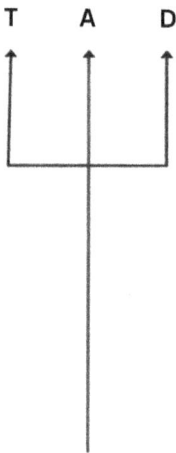

T - Transparency
A - Autonomy
D - Decision Making

TAD TRIDENT

If we look to history, it is evident that the nature of weapons used in the past closely matched the dynamics of the collective goals they chased. Cavemen used flints and spears for hunting and food gathering; medieval rulers used swords, daggers and bows for building kingdoms; and colonial forces used guns and bombs for acquiring territories and subjugating people.

However, as a contemporary leader, regardless of your profession and in whichever institution you're working, you require the Trident to conquer your collective goals. Certainly, you don't want to acquire territories and carve out kingdoms with swords and daggers, but deep down we all have an unquenching appetite to build expansive empires in our respective domains—whether it is business, education, arts or social service. We all desire our projects, institutions, firms, brands and finances to grow and expand to mountainous heights and oceanic depths. Your success thus hinges on your willingness to employ this powerful trident and on how effectively you can leverage its three prongs—transparency, autonomy and decision making (TAD).

Let us discuss the relevance of each prong before we decode their concerted power.

Prong 1: Transparency

On April 10, 2015, a special CBI court held Ramalinga Raju, founder of Satyam Computer Services, guilty of an accounting scam worth ₹7,000 crores and sentenced him to 7 years in jail. But in 2008, exactly 7 years before his conviction, his firm was the 4th largest IT conglomerate and its revenue crossed $2 billion. The company even bagged contracts as the official IT service provider for the FIFA World Cups in 2010 and 2014. Raju was India's poster boy and rubbed shoulders with top CEOs and politicians. He even once made a famous statement that his journey felt like he was riding a tiger and did not know how to get off without being eaten.

Unexpectedly, on January 7, 2009, he sent an email to Securities and Exchange Board of India (SEBI) and the stock exchanges, confessing to inflating the revenue and profits of the company. Within three days, Satyam's shares abruptly fell to ₹11.50 compared to a high of ₹544 in 2008. Although his confession triggered the firm's demise, the root cause for the collapse was a lack of transparency. All the key stakeholders—the board of directors, investors and employees—had no notion about the fraud brewing internally.

Transparency builds a kind of default peer monitoring mechanism. Moreover, transparency fosters accountability in the system, which is vital to accomplishing your team goals in the earliest possible time frame. When employees know their responsibilities, they become more accountable and compete to complete their individual assignments. Assigning responsibilities to subordinates in a transparent manner also makes use of the optimum use of the workforce and of resources, and dramatically improves the system's efficiency.

Besides, institutionalized transparency also ensures that employees don't feel alienated or engage in blame-shifting games. It also prevents nepotism, favouritism, Machiavellianism and back-stabbing—the poisonous weeds that breed in systems that are run in a murky manner.

Prong 2: Autonomy

Freedom to do one's job, with minimal interference from those higher up in the hierarchy, adds unique joy and a sense of pride in the profession. Everyone loves freedom and a secure personal space to incubate brilliant ideas, showcase authentic genius, and create their magnum opus.

Don't you?

Everyone wants a bare minimum guarantee of autonomy while operating in order to unleash peak performance. And, like transparency, autonomy also builds accountability. Isn't it true that when employees are not given enough of a free hand to execute a task, they tend to pass the buck to others and refuse to take responsibility for professional blunders?

It is for these reasons that granting adequate authority to the people working under you is so important. While delegating work and responsibilities to your subordinates, you can follow the *don't put square pegs in round holes* technique. In the corporate world, a marketing expert does not look after the finances of the company, or the person who is adept at financial management is not involved in formulating policies and strategies for the firm. Similarly, you should also first assess an individual's aptitude and then allot work based on their inherent talent and calibre. The direct consequence of such a decentralized administration is that you can free up time for yourself for the key roles of monitoring, supervision, evaluation and course correction, which are vital for the perfect execution of your institutional goals.

Autonomy is a critical prong of TAD. Companies like Nike, Amazon and Starbucks achieve their milestones not because of an autocratic CEO or dictatorial directors. They do it in a democratic way. The head of the HR department has enough liberty to recruit employees, the marketing head has the leeway to create innovative ad campaigns, the finance section can plan debt-reduction strategies and the customer department can devise its own methods to enhance client satisfaction. And that's why Nike is selling 26 pairs of shoes per second, Amazon is delivering 1.6 million packages a day, and Starbucks is making 4 billion cups of coffee every year. Every successful firm uses autonomy as a necessary brick to construct a wall of stability and prosperity. It encourages employee engagement and gives them the opportunity to showcase initiative and leadership.

Prong 3: Decision Making

An extraordinary man was born in 1847 in Milan, Ohio. He worked as a telegraph operator before eventually registering 1,093 US patents in his name and emerging as one of the greatest inventors on this planet. His inventions include the phonograph, the motion picture camera, and the light bulb—incredible discoveries that revolutionized society forever.

His name is Thomas Edison. We are well acquainted with his inveterate commitment, unbending will and untiring persistence; but the real reason for his spectacular achievements was his bold decision to quit his job as a telegraph operator in 1876. He decided to build the first-ever industrial research lab in Menlo Park, New Jersey. Menlo Park made a genius out of him.

This is one way to sharpen the prong of decision making. You must make prompt decisions when you are absolutely sure about what you intend to do in life. There is no point in vacillating when you get a pathbreaking idea. You ought to act before the inertias of dilemma, procrastination and fear of failure douse your spark.

The second way to hone decision making is to employ the prong of autonomy. Devolve enough authority to your subordinates so that they can make their own decisions. People around you are equally competent and mature and will make wise decisions. Edison followed this method too. At Menlo Park, he was not the only one who decided on research experiments to be conducted. Instead, teams of passionate scientists were given the freedom to choose their individual projects. He called it Collective Intelligence. Everyone had enough latitude to explore within the domain of their expertise, with the common goal of producing trailblazing inventions.

Decision making in a democratic way not only brings in people with diverse backgrounds and cultures to a common platform and enriches the existing knowledge pool, but also encourages them to work for team goals with more dedication and fervour. Organizations that use this strategy have considerable advantage over those working in tight silos and tend to achieve their set milestones at a rapid pace.

After decoding the power of the three individual prongs of the TAD trident, let us see how the combined might of all three is indispensable in accomplishing collective goals.

ACCOMPLISHING COLLECTIVE GOALS THROUGH TAD

Consider a typical household milieu. Every day, family members do a great deal of work in the house—cooking, cleaning, laundry, grocery purchase, grooming and educating children, financial planning, recreation and entertainment. Which member gets what responsibility is invariably decided through mutual understanding or a division of labor—the erstwhile concept followed since the Vedic period.

Now, whether or not the different family members complete their work on time ultimately boils down to the degree of conscious and deliberate efforts they are making to foster transparency, autonomy and strong decision making. If household members are not transparent in sharing their mutual expectations, or they fail to provide adequate independence to each other, or they do not simplify the workload through a clear-cut demarcation of responsibilities, things will undoubtedly go awry. Efforts will be futile and work will remain incomplete.

This is just one system. Take another closely-bound system: a sports team! For illustration, I cite here the example of the Brazilian soccer team. Anyone with some idea about soccer and an interest in watching it will agree that they are the undisputed champions of the game.

What makes them so unique?

The ability of this team to create magical moves on the soccer field, to keep spectators spellbound, and to win championship after championship, can be ascribed to just one entity, the TAD trident. Let us examine how they exploit this.

All eleven players in this team have different individual roles and responsibilities. The strikers are required for scoring goals, midfielders are essential for playmaking and orchestrating fine passes, defenders are meant to fortify against the attacking opponent, and the goalkeeper is the lynchpin securing the goal post. Each one of them is a specialist. Yet, if midfielders are not given enough autonomy to craft various tactical moves, or the strikers do not have transparency and good chemistry, or the goalkeeper fails to make a firm decision about when and where to move while blocking the shot, the virtuosity of all the individual players will fail to produce collective magic.

Without TAD, these players wouldn't produce marvellous performances that delight spectators watching from the stands. Minus these elements, the soccer field will host a chaotic scene, with random players roaming in frustration for 90 minutes, finally inviting the wrath of irate spectators.

Takeaways

- Team spirit is a critical atom of The Graphene Mentality. It provides a strong edifice for building resilience, firmness and adaptability.

- Prolific performance in whatever field you choose— business, engineering, medicine or sports—depends more on team effort rather than individual brilliance.

- Cultivate team spirit by embracing the twin MATs.

- Deploy the TAD Trident to achieve your collective goals.

PENCIL WORK

- Answer this question honestly: are you a bootstrapper who believes in working alone, which is heroic but foolhardy? Or are you a team player who actively leverages the talent and skills of your colleagues to achieve your individual as well as collective goals?

- Identify 5-6 people (they could be your peers, friends, family members or mentors) whose vibes strongly resonate with your frequency, and who are pivotal to the realization of your splendid goals. Write down their names so that you can meet them often. They are integral members of your small but effective team.

III.

Ignite
and
Recharge

In this section, you will learn certain strategies and routines to ignite and recharge your Graphene Mentality.

IGNITE

'Who knows why some words ignite the hearts of some readers while others are like wet matches that won't light.'

– Phil Cousineau

CHAPTER 8

Communication Skills
Igniting the Graphene Mentality

What you will learn in this chapter

- How communication skills ignite atoms of your Graphene Mentality.
- What are the two foundational pillars of building communication skills?
- What is the LISTEN strategy to improve your listening ability?

Almost 70,000 years ago, Homo sapiens displaced all other human species that existed, such as Neanderthals, Homo erectus and Homo rudolfensis. They spread to different continents and settled there due to their unique prowess and dominated the earth for many millennia (and still continue at an unrivaled pace).

Any idea what that unique prowess is?

Well, it is their communication skills! They could compete with and eliminate all other species because they possessed the prodigious ability to communicate among themselves. And by virtue of this uncanny acumen, they could forge large groups and alliances. No other human species had that advantage because they could never gain prominent mastery over language, as Homo sapiens did. Homo sapiens began communicating to alert their commune members about threats like lions and tigers, gradually used it to gossip and spread rumors about others, and eventually evolved it to create myths, fictions, legends and religions. This way, they could not only build solid associations but also succeed in motivating others to fight against different species for their survival.

Evolutionary psychologist Robin Dunbar expounded the gossiping and grooming hypothesis to explain that unlike primates, such as apes and monkeys, who created cohesive groups by grooming fellow members by scratching their backs, removing fleas and feeding, we resorted to gossiping to maintain our larger groups. This is why primates are still scratching each other's backs while we've built colossal business conglomerates and supercomputers.

In his book *Sapiens: A Brief History of Humankind*, Yuval Noah Harari writes that the deftness to conjure myths and fictions through gossip allowed Sapiens to cooperate flexibly in large numbers. Ants and bees can also work together in huge numbers, but they do so in a very rigid manner and only with close relatives. Wolves and chimpanzees cooperate far more flexibly than ants do, but they can do so only with the small number of others of their kind that they know intimately. Sapiens can cooperate in extremely flexible ways with a countless number of strangers.

Sapiens thus used communication to ignite their atoms of team spirit, flexibility and resilience, and achieved their common goal of survival.

In the 21st century, more than for survival, we use communication to propel us towards our goals and objectives. We communicate to influence people to vote for us and win elections, to persuade people to buy iPhones and smart watches, to seduce travelers to visit Cyprus, Dubai or Disneyland, and to motivate players to win championship after championship. The metaverse has taken us to a different level, where we can perform tons of activities together even if thousands of miles separate us. We can schedule meetings to discuss our work agenda, speak with a doctor about our illness, gossip and play games with our friends, celebrate festivals with our family members, and maybe someday, if technology continues to progress like this, we'll be romancing with our partners.

Communication has unlocked unprecedented opportunities, and honing your skill and expertise in this segment is the single most effective strategy to compete and stay ahead. When the mission is the same and the objective is common, communication skills become a key catalyst in igniting all the atoms of The Graphene Mentality—firmness, flexibility, resilience and team spirit.

Two foundational pillars are critical to building remarkable communication skills. If you want to sculpt monuments of success in your respective spheres, you must ensure that these pillars are sturdy.

PILLAR 1: AOS—(THE) ART OF SPEAKING

The art of speaking does not merely connect people, regions or countries; it integrates the entire globe and all the 8 million species inhabiting it. AOS, whether it has a soft tone or an animated pitch, is a powerful tool to galvanize people if the words are chosen carefully. What I mean is that speech should not offend the sentiments of the listener, as it can have a lasting impact on their psychology and perception.

AOS helps to reap profound gains—be it ramping up sales in business, scoring political mileage in elections through high-decibel rallies, or building interpersonal relations in society. Achievers across all these domains have one thing in common—they are terrific communicators with sublime public speaking acumen.

Apple was in shambles, on the verge of bankruptcy, when Steve Jobs returned in 1997. The company was mocked heavily in business parleys and its computers were a laughingstock, often labelled as "toys." Employees were morose and cynical, casting doubts on the firm's future prospects. But that was only until Jobs courageously revived the company's fortunes by spearheading a huge marketing campaign through the commercial "To the crazy ones." It was a short video showing iconic personalities such as Albert Einstein, Muhammad Ali, Pablo Picasso and Mahatma Gandhi, with this narration in the background:

"Here's to the crazy ones. The misfits. The rebels. The troublemakers. The round pegs in square holes. The ones who see things differently. They're not fond of rules, and they have no respect for the status quo. You can quote them, disagree with them, glorify or vilify them. But the only thing you can't do is ignore them. Because they change things, they push the human race forward. And while some may see them as the crazy ones, we see genius. Because the people who are crazy enough to think they can change the world are the ones who do."

This commercial, which ended with the tagline "Think different" written just below the Apple logo, changed the company's history forever. It not only captivated consumers and catapulted the sales of Apple products, but also ignited the collective spirit, firm belief and resilience of all its employees.

The debate over who the real architect of the marketing campaign was is still not settled and many narratives credit different creative artists involved in this project. In no uncertain terms, there could have been many navigators and engineers, but there was only one captain of the ship. And he was none other than the charismatic and visionary Steve Jobs. His AOS was impeccable. He kept it simple and delivered his message in tune with the problems and needs of his audiences. Throughout his career, he leveraged AOS as a business marketing strategy, especially when launching breakthrough products like the iPhone in 2007.

"You will never walk alone!" is the famous anthem of the Liverpool Football Club, sung together since 1963. Whether the club wins championships or not, this song echoes rhythmically and synchronously every time players in red shirts march into the stadium. It not only mobilizes the club's fans but also ignites team spirit and resilience among players, powering them to score goal after goal.

That is the power of AOS!

MODES OF AOS

AOS has three principal modes—non-verbal, verbal and written. And it ignites your atoms when it is flawless in all these three modes.

A. Non-verbal

Everyone would agree that Usain Bolt is among the most legendary athletes in the history of sports. He asserted his supremacy in his game by winning gold medals in all the events he participated in across three consecutive Olympics.

Though his perseverance and discipline in training were unparalleled, his clear advantage over other competitors was due to his body language before every event. At the starting line-up before each race, his confident smile and blazing eyes differentiated him from the nervous faces beside him. He connected with spectators in a manner no one ever could match. And who can forget his signature pose after every victory, in which he leaned back with one arm to the sky and the other pulled back by his ears with a bent elbow, which made his body look like the shape of a lightning bolt.

Expressive body language is a game-changer. The success of any team, whether it is the Chelsea Football Club, a satellite launch team, or a musical band about to perform live on the stage, can be predicted by just looking at the faces of the team members.

The bottom line is that body language—positive or negative—predicts outcomes depending on how you present yourself while performing for your coveted goal. A robust, impactful, vibrant body language sets the stage for glory. On the contrary, feeble and timid body language is a harbinger of doom.

Social psychologist Amy Cuddy once gave a TED Talk on the subject, "Your Body Language May Shape Who You Are." In her speech, Cuddy explains that it is not just our minds that change our bodies, our bodies can change our minds, too. "Can you fake it to make it?" she asks this question to all audiences at the beginning of the lecture. Then, she recommends this strategy of fake it till you make it, emphasizing that adopting a dominant posture and powerful gestures, even though fake, can bring about positive outcomes. It radically reconfigures your thought patterns and influences your behavior in a significant way.

Her argument is not without merit. Ray Birdwhistell, an eminent anthropologist, pioneered the study of non-verbal communication called kinesics. Through his extensive study, he deciphered that we make and recognize around 250,000 facial expressions. A huge number. And not only this but there are also other subtle non-verbal cues that are directly responsible for 65% of our communication. Upright posture, appropriate hand movements and optimum eye contact signals a lot about our attitude, interest, competence, comfort, and so on. And that's what makes all the difference while you're interacting with someone. It engages your listeners and sets the tempo for an interesting and inclusive conversation.

B. Verbal

Spoken words may account for just 35% of your communication but they can have a much greater impact when articulated effectively. When a captain motivates their teammates with an explosive cry, it immediately triggers a surge of adrenaline and can cause goosebumps. Encouraging words like, "Come on guys, buck up!" radiate positivity, hope, belief and courage among the team members. Collective morale and resilience of the team depend on the choice of words uttered by the leader during crunch moments.

If you have any doubts regarding this, read this excerpt from one of the greatest speeches ever made by any leader to inspire a country's citizens in the face of one of the worst catastrophes of the 20th century.

"We shall go on to the end, we shall fight in France, we shall fight on the seas and oceans, we shall fight with growing confidence and growing strength in the air, we shall defend our island, whatever the cost may be. We shall fight on the beaches; we shall fight on the landing grounds. We shall fight in the fields and in the streets, we shall fight in the hills; we shall never surrender, and even if, which I do not for a moment believe, this island or a large part of it were subjugated and starving, then our Empire beyond the seas, armed and guarded by the British fleet, would carry on the struggle, until, in God's good time, the new world, with all its power and might, steps forth to the rescue and the liberation of the old."

During World War II, Winston Churchill ignited his countrymen through such powerful speeches and rekindled their morale to fight against the Nazis, altering the course of the war in favor of the Allied forces in a decisive manner.

Similar to Churchill, on August 28, 1963, Martin Luther King Jr. delivered his famous "I Have a Dream" speech in front of the Lincoln Memorial, with almost 200,000 people gathering to hear him. He begins with:

"Let us not wallow in the valley of despair, I say to you today, my friends. So even though we face the difficulties of today and tomorrow, I still have a dream. It is a dream deeply rooted in the American dream. I have a dream that one day, this nation will rise up and live out the true meaning of its creed: 'We hold these truths to be self-evident, that all men are created equal.' I have a dream that one day, on the red hills of Georgia, the sons of former slaves and the sons of former slave owners will be able to sit down together at the table of brotherhood. I have a dream that my four little children will one day live in a nation where they will not be judged by the color of their skin but by the content of their character. I have a dream today!"

This speech marshalled people towards the common goal to achieve justice and equality for Black people in American society. It ultimately culminated in the passing of The Civil Rights Act of 1964, which banned discrimination in employment and public accommodations based on race, color, religion or national origin. It could not have been made possible without the power and intensity embedded in King Jr.'s speech. His cadence and tactical repetition of *I have a dream* at the beginning of every sentence elevated the soul of everyone in the audience.

Apart from the atoms of resilience and team spirit, verbal speech also ignites the atom of firmness. Firmness in initiating something or persisting with it once you have initiated it requires clear and explicit communication backed by commanding language. Simply replacing "We will think about it" with "We will do it" makes a lot of difference. It helps build the conviction required to pursue any project, agenda or mission.

C. Written Language

What you write on a piece of paper not only reflects your intention but also constantly exhorts you to cling to your priceless goal, like a kangaroo does to her baby. When you feel like abandoning your dreams because of daunting odds, looking at your customized, bold mission statement restores your zeal. Spoken words inspire instantly, but written words inspire perpetually.

History is abundant with examples of iconic people who believed in the power of strong written language. Many among them even invented personalized quotes to instruct themselves that they were meant to stay and not surrender. Some of these quotes are:

"If my mind can conceive it, and my heart can believe it, then I can achieve it."

— Muhammad Ali

"Genius is 99% perspiration and 1% inspiration."

— Thomas Edison

"Arise, awake, and stop not till the goal is achieved."

— Swami Vivekananda

"That which does not kill us, makes us stronger."

— Friedrich Nietzsche

"Impossible is the word in the dictionary of fools."

— Napoleon

"The more you sweat in peace, the less you bleed in war."

— Norman Schwarzkopf

These famous quotes have emboldened the people who invented them and continue to spur millions of others in playgrounds, auditoriums, libraries, classrooms, laboratories and conference halls.

I'm not prodding you to imitate their words blindly because the situations and adversities you face might be different from what these eminent people faced. You can design your own mission statement in the language that reflects your unique challenges and circumstances.

Yet I can offer you one hack: you should make it as precise and vivid as possible. Don't make it insipid and vague. Use vibrant and specific language to enable you to forge an instant emotional connection with your content. Instead of simply writing "resilience," if you write, "I shall bounce back, no matter how hapless I am rendered by the failures," it makes your statement more dynamic. If in lieu of writing "team spirit," you write, "I will cooperate with my colleagues and never work in a selfish way," you would succeed in cultivating team spirit. Similarly, instead of just stating "firmness" as a virtue, if you make a strong affirmation that "I shall not relinquish my goal even if I am hammered by multiple adversities," it will infuse greater strength in you to persist with your chosen goal.

PILLAR 2: AOL—(THE) ART OF LISTENING

"I know that you believe you understand what you think I said, but I'm not sure you realize that what you heard is not what I meant."

– Robert McCloskey

Whether it is Martin Luther King Jr. who delivered the "I have a dream" speech, or Abraham Lincoln who articulated "Government of the people, by the people, for the people" during the Gettysburg address; whether it is Winston Churchill's inspiring call of "We shall fight on the beaches" during WWII, or Swami Vivekananda advocating a fusion of the East's spiritualism and the West's materialism during the Chicago World's Parliament of Religions in 1893, one common attribute of all these leaders was their strong AOS.

However, the contours of leadership remain incomplete without AOL.

The iconic American television and radio host Larry King once said, "I remind myself every morning: nothing I say this day will teach me anything. So, if I'm going to learn, I must do it by listening."

The hallmark of great communicators is not just their eloquence, but their focused and empathetic listening as well. Leadership is not only the animated and manufactured speech you make to your team; it is also about being open-minded while listening to the opinions and feedback of your teammates. Triumph does not lie in chest-thumping and making grandiose gestures after hitting milestones. It lies in your patience to listen to your critics during failures.

The career of legendary cricketer Mahendra Singh Dhoni aptly embodies this. He succeeded in his career because he was calm and listened to his teammates. He had tremendous AOL, which imparted so much confidence among his players that they could walk up to him and share their inputs without hesitation. Through his remarkable listening ability, he built a prolific team that pulled off victories in three ICC finals—an unprecedented achievement that no team captain has replicated yet.

FIVE DIVIDENDS OF AOL

The miraculous power of AOL lies in its five glorious dividends.

First and foremost, it allows you to GROW. You can assimilate a lot of knowledge just by listening. Unlike reading, for which you must first purchase the book and then make an effort to read it, listening is the most cost-effective way to learn. It demands no money and requires just your attention and empathy towards the speaker. That is why all profound and knowledgeable people are great listeners.

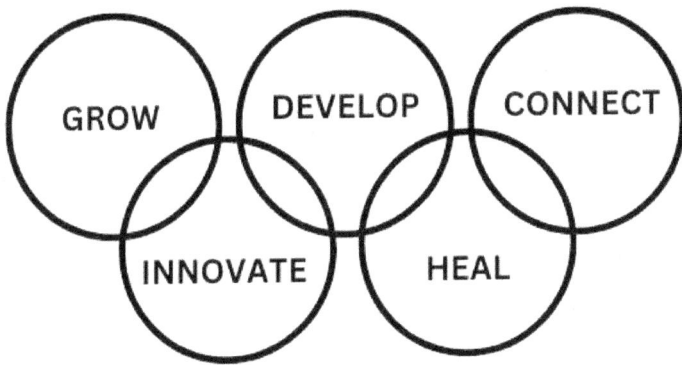

FIVE DIVIDENDS OF AOL

Second, it enables you to DEVELOP. Attentive listening engages those critical parts of the brain that develop your focus, attention span and concentration. If you don't believe this, make an endeavor to remain silent for 24 hours and listen to whatever is being said and fed to your ears. You will be amazed to notice a sharp improvement in your attention span and concentration.

Third, listening is the best way to CONNECT. Compassionate listening helps convey to the speaker that the listener really cares about his or her opinion and arguments, eventually establishing an intimate connection between them. The art of listening is a great relationship builder.

Fourth, it empowers people to INNOVATE. It has been observed that organizations where employers are keen to listen to employees are more innovative overall. This is because brilliant ideas from employees flow seamlessly into the system only when they are convinced that they are being heard effectively by the employer.

Fifth, it allows people to HEAL. When you listen to the problems and sufferings of others, you give them an opportunity to mitigate their grief. Take the example of the healthcare industry. More than the skill and expertise of the treating physician, it is their empathetic listening that heals the patient's illness. In outpatient departments, the time spent per patient is more important than the number of patients seen per hour. A patient's satisfaction counts more than the hospital statistics.

You might now question, if the art of listening has so many fabulous dividends, then why are the majority of people not good listeners?

The explanation lies in these stumbling blocks.

Stumbling blocks

Essentially, there are four stumbling blocks to effective listening—poor attention, pressure of speech, prejudices and paranoia (the 4Ps):

P1: Poor attention span. The rate at which we think is faster than the rate at which we register spoken words, creating a lot of spare time in our brain, which allows for random thoughts that impede effective listening.

P2: Pressure of speech. It is a behavioral anomaly wherein the person who is listening interrupts the speaker because of the irresistible urge to prove his or her point.

P3: Prejudices. The listener has a preconceived notion, bias or judgement against the speaker and is reluctant to listen.

P4: Paranoia. The listener is paranoid and thinks that if they listen for a prolonged time, they will be perceived as silent.

To overcome these stumbling blocks and improve your listening ability, I have devised this LISTEN strategy.

LISTEN to LISTEN

L: Listen with a beginner's ear. Do not get driven by the pressure of speech and interrupt the speaker before they are finished.

I: Impartial listening. Discard inherent bias (due to conflicting ideology, opinion and beliefs) against the speaker.

S: Silence. Follow a ritual of silence one day a week. It will enhance your focus and concentration.

T: Try to look directly into the eyes of the person speaking.

E: Emotions. Make a conscious effort to understand the emotions behind the speech. Do not just focus on the information. This will help you to engage with the speaker.

N: No gadgets. Eliminate the excessive use of gadgets as it helps in reducing major distractions.

The time to LISTEN cannot be more important now. We are heading into a massive listening crisis triggered by our overpowering urge to speak and seek validation for our arguments. Cultivating AOL is the only way to curb this trend.

We need to understand that when we become a good listener, we can begin to acknowledge our faults and weaknesses as pointed out by others and we can start making conscious efforts to rectify and improve ourselves. We become more FLEXIBLE. If AOS has the potential to ignite the atoms of firmness and resilience, then AOL is the ideal strategy to ignite the atom of flexibility.

Takeaways

- The power of communication ignites the atoms of flexibility, firmness, resilience and team spirit.

- It has two foundational pillars: AOS and AOL.

- To sharpen your AOS, make yourself proficient in its three principal modes: Non-verbal, verbal and written.

- To amplify your AOL, practice LISTEN strategy.

PENCIL WORK

- Write down one aspect of your communication skills in which you believe you are lacking, and then work hard to build upon it.

- Mark one day a week in your calendar when you will remain silent and listen to your employees, colleagues, spouse, kids, parents or personal coach. Preferably choose a working day because it is usually when you're instigated by your impulses, insecurities and ego to make your point to the people around you.

RECHARGE

'If you neglect to recharge a battery, it dies. And if you run full speed ahead without stopping for water, you lose momentum to finish the race.'

– Oprah Winfrey

CHAPTER 9

Fitness, Diet and Sleep
Recharging the Graphene Mentality

What you will learn in this chapter

- How fitness, diet and sleep recharge your mentality and deliver round-the-clock energy to your targeted efforts.

If effective communication skills can ignite you and your team towards a common goal, fitness, diet and sleep can recharge your Graphene Mentality and deliver consistent energy to your efforts. When you're disciplined in these three key elements of your daily routine, you feel more light, energetic and focused throughout the day.

At 38, the endurance and stamina of Virat Kohli, the legendary cricketer, and Novak Djokovic, the talismanic player, rival those of an 18-year-old athlete. They credit their resilience to compete in highly intense games, and their flexibility to perform and excel in challenging circumstances, to fitness, diet and sleep. While their competitors are equally talented and skilful, what sets these athletes apart is their commitment to follow a disciplined routine in these aspects. That's why they maintain their perfect shape and play without much discomfort or injuries, while their competitors suffer from muscle and ligament tears.

Indeed, this troika holds tremendous significance in every field of life. Start implementing today and within a month, you'll see incredible results in your energy, positivity and overall outlook. You will be able to handle adversities without buckling under pressure, will make quick decisions more confidently, and will manage your emotions better, which will make you work free of stress towards your set targets.

Super Producers in all sectors have only one secret to their perennial enthusiasm—they recharge themselves with this troika every day. Jack Dorsey, former CEO of Twitter and Square, attributes his success in these two prolific companies to his strict regimen of diet, fitness and sleep. When asked about the stress of running two companies, Dorsey said he views it as a motivator and an opportunity to keep learning. He admitted that it had also been a catalyst for making significant changes in his personal life. "When I went back to Twitter and took on the second job, I got super serious about meditation, and I got serious about dedicating a lot more time and energy to working out and staying physically healthy and looking more critically at my diet," he confessed.

Now, let's dig through the recharging potential of all three powerful elements.

FITNESS: THE FIRST RECHARGE

Our workout regime and overall fitness impacts our energy levels, body language, thought pattern and mood. When we sweat out in the morning, our commitment and intensity at our workplace is phenomenal. When we skip it, we become lethargic and our affinity towards profession diminishes, depleting our work productivity. Our professional output is directly proportional to how much sincere efforts we take to move our body during precious morning hours. Yet we tend to be erratic in sticking to a fitness schedule, robbing ourselves of the opportunity to recharge and refuel our engine of performance.

To stay on track, I have devised my own weekly schedule. It creates a sort of moral obligation to follow it religiously, ensuring that I remain charged up throughout the day.

This is my weekly workout schedule.

Day	Activity	Result
Monday	Cardio (Running/Cycling/Swimming)	Endurance, Speed
Tuesday	2.5 km warmup + Calisthenics	Strength, Stability
Wednesday	HIIT (High intensity interval training)	Endurance, Speed & Intensity
Thursday	2.5 km warmup + Calisthenics	Strength, Stability
Friday	Cardio (Running/Cycling/Swimming)	Endurance, Speed
Saturday	Yoga	Flexibility
Sunday	Recovery and Rest	

Weekly Workout Schedule
* Two compulsory rituals
  - MS Protocol – Take MS (Massage and Steam therapy) once or twice a week.
  - Mind Training – 10-15 minutes of mind training every day after workout.

I have tried to make it as holistic and comprehensive as possible. Every activity in the regimen is incorporated with a specific motive. Running fosters endurance, HIIT brings in speed and intensity, calisthenics builds strength and stability, yoga imparts flexibility, massage and steam therapy helps in fast recovery from injuries, and mind training ensures mental resilience.

ENERGY WHEEL:
EIGHT MAGICAL BENEFITS OF WORKOUT

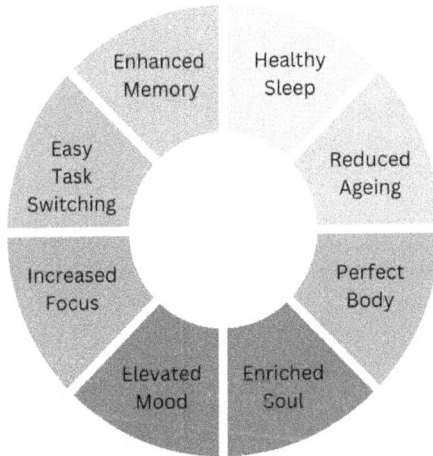

Enhanced Memory

Healthy Sleep

Easy Task Switching

Reduced Ageing

Increased Focus

Perfect Body

Elevated Mood

Enriched Soul

ENERGY WHEEL

I have tried my best to distil all the magical benefits of doing regular workout into this Energy Wheel. Memorize it, use it as your screen saver, or paste it in your bedroom at a prominent place, so that every morning when you look at it, you push your will and motivation on track before it gets derailed. Do whatever works for you. These benefits cover three essential dimensions of your life: cognitive, physical and spiritual. By recharging your body, mind and soul, you can align all three to work in unison in pursuit of your goals.

Cognitive benefits	Process
Increased focus Enhanced memory Easy task switching	Diminished activity in the default mode network (DMN) of the brain which is responsible for "monkey mind" and ceaseless rumination on the past and present. Release of Brain-Derived Neurotrophic Factor (BDNF), which triggers neurogenesis. Increase in volume of hippocampus—the memory and learning centre of the brain.
Physical benefits	
Perfect body	Running burns belly fat.
Reduced ageing Healthy sleep	Running leads to increased telomerase activity. This enzyme maintains the length of telomere-cap over chromosomes, which protects them from damage and prevents ageing. Serotonin release reduces anxiety and ensures sound sleep.
Spiritual benefits	
Elevated mood Enriched soul	Due to the release of feel-good hormones such as endorphins and endocannabinoids.

While designing your weekly workout schedule, you need not imitate my regime in a sacrosanct manner. You can tweak it by including physical activities that you like doing, and that give you an instant kick.

But don't forget to add these two essentials of composite fitness—the MS protocol and an exclusive Mind Training.

MS PROTOCOL

MS combines the two most potent rituals of recovery ever known—massage therapy and steam therapy. Booking a 45-minute massage session (hire the professionals, not the fraudsters and bogus practitioners operating from dingy clusters in your town), followed by steam bath, is a revitalizing experience. It has some overt and instant benefits such as reducing stiffness, improving flexibility, reducing stress (due to the release of endorphins), helping your skin glow (by enhancing blood circulation to the skin), and boosting immunity (by activating white blood cells).

More specifically, MS protocol is necessary because it maintains your motivation and sustains interest in your physical activity. Isn't it so common to be initially excited for workouts before they become a boring part of your routine? You start despising the thing you liked the most.

This natural decline in enthusiasm is an inevitable product of tired muscles, injured ligaments and stiff tendons—the collateral damage done during exhaustive sessions. Your jaded body relays negative feedback to your brain, affecting the motivational pathways in the limbic system. Taking the first step out of bed becomes the most challenging task in the world. As soon as you wake up in the morning, the first thing you discover is a heavy body that behaves like a lifeless boulder. The mind too gets bulky, dragging you back into the inertia of fear and procrastination. And then you feel as though you need a massive crane to lift you up and get you moving.

Practicing MS ritual after every laborious session helps rejuvenate fatigued muscles, stimulates the repair of strained ligaments and tendons, and makes you more kinetic and buoyant for the next session. When you rise in the morning, your body doesn't feel like a heavy boulder requiring any sort of machinery to move. Instead, it becomes light like cumulonimbus clouds, as if you're floating in the air, ready to conquer exquisite horizons. Your mind gets rid of redundant stuff and you're ready to restart with greater efficiency and more power, like an automobile that delivers better mileage and a smooth ride after its mandatory service. The moment engine oil and lubricants are put into the car, it feels brand new, with steering, suspension, brakes and pickup operating flawlessly.

To put it simply, massage and steam-induced recovery of the body and mind eventually crafts a revival of interest in the physical activity that you're fond of doing. The lost love, affection and longing for your favourite workout is found again. And consequently, you make yourself more consistent in adhering to your customized fitness schedule.

MIND TRAINING

Besides MS protocol, taking out some time for your mind training should be your top-most priority. Because our mind is constantly agitated due to chaotic hustles of daily life. We need to make it stable and peaceful. And there are plenty of exercises to do that. Mindfulness, Yoga and breathing exercises are few of them.

Here, I will tell you about mindfulness without delving into the others because that's the most powerful amongst all.

WHAT IS MINDFULNESS?

Mindfulness is the practice of being present in the moment. Initially, you can start with 5-10 minutes of session immediately after morning workout, concentrating on breathing in and breathing out. Gradually, you can build it to focus on the essence of every activity that you're doing—allowing your body, mind and soul to feel the vibrations emanating from it. When brushing your teeth, focus on the sensations produced while you're rubbing soft bristles against your enamels in all four quadrants of your oral cavity. When taking a bath, immerse yourself in the pleasure of feeling the texture and temperature (warm or cold) of water drops. When you button up your shirt or tie your shoelaces, gently bring all your attention onto your fingers doing this rote movement for you. While reading, feel the beauty of meaning that each sentence crystallizes for you, and while listening, surrender yourself to the delight of absorbing the speaker's words without any prejudice or expert comments.

Obviously, when you rewire your brain to respond and live in this novel way, you will be mauled by intermittent streams of weird thoughts that originate from nowhere. But it's important to be non-judgemental towards the patterns of thoughts as they arise, and welcome both pleasant as well as unpleasant ones, clean as well as dirty, and benign as well as malignant. Identify them, label them, but don't react to them.

This is mindfulness. It's different from meditation.

Meditation is all about centering on your breath, a sound, a flame, or any specific object that is within the palpable reach of your senses. It is practiced for brief periods, maybe 30 or 45 minutes, where you deliberately try to deflect all kinds of negative thoughts sneaking into your mind. And there is no guarantee that you won't have bizarre thoughts once your meditation session is over.

Meditation teaches you to avoid hostile and evil thoughts, which you can never avoid in real life, while mindfulness allows you to accept and adapt to them. Meditation trains you to live in the present moment for a short period, while mindfulness trains you to live in the present moment forever, irrespective of the nature of the task being performed. A meditation session requires extreme calm and serenity, while mindfulness can be practiced even when driving through traffic. All you need to do is to appreciate the sound waves emitted by the horns of the vehicles passing by your side.

Mindfulness is an advanced form of meditation.

The essence of the wisdom of mindfulness is to acknowledge and embrace thoughts and things as they are until their impact becomes ineffective. If you try to repel, it will keep hitting back. It is a universal truth that those who have successfully overcome negativity, worries and mental agonies of past traumatic events have done it by adapting themselves through mindfulness, and not by choosing an escape route. As Lord Krishna aptly said to Arjuna, "Actionless-ness cannot be attained by forsaking actions."

HOW DOES MINDFULNESS WORK?

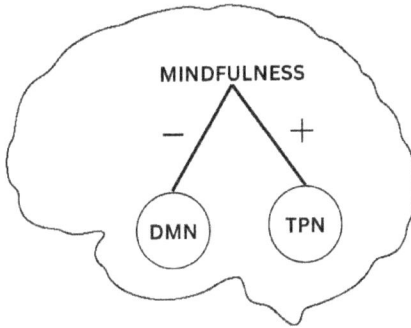

DMN = DEFAULT MODE NETWORK

↓

- Monkey mind
- Anxiety
- Distress

TPN = TASK POSITIVE NETWORK

↓

- Stable mind
- Peace
- Happiness

Mindfulness shuts off DMN (default mode network) and switches on TPN (task positive network). DMN comprises the medial prefrontal cortex and amygdala—areas of the brain that are often associated with rumination and random thoughts about the past and future. Studies show that nearly half of our waking hours are spent in this mode, with 80% of our thoughts being negative in nature. Only 20% of our thoughts tend to focus on positive events and pleasant memories. Our mind is like a perfect time machine, constantly travelling between the past and future.

On the contrary, TPN or task positive network comprises the lateral prefrontal cortex and hippocampus. It gets activated when we do focused tasks which demand our attention. When we practice mindfulness, we activate TPN, which automatically blunts DMN response. A surge in TPN activity results in a stable, less wandering, mind, eventually leading to substantial peace and happiness.

Through a seminal study, Dr Sara Lazar of Harvard Medical School validated the neuroscience behind mindfulness. She divided her candidates into two groups. One group was subjected to mindfulness for eight weeks, while the other was excluded from the intervention. When she compared brain images (MRI scans) of both groups, she observed that candidates who underwent mindfulness showed increased grey matter in the hippocampus and lateral prefrontal cortex (TPN), along with considerable shrinkage in the size of the amygdala (DMN). However, the candidates not subjected to mindfulness showed no significant change in the brain's grey matter.

The amygdala is the brain's emotional centre and is responsible for the fight or flight response whenever we face a difficult situation. It is the amygdala that sets off our pounding chest, palpitations and sweating before high tension moments, whether it is a PowerPoint presentation, skydiving or surfing. Its shrinkage consequent to mindfulness is the principal reason for the dramatic reduction in anxiety during stressful events.

Dr Lazar's study debunks the notion that brain size does not change much after a certain age. In reality, the brain experiences neuroplasticity throughout life and can be rewired daily by practicing mindfulness. The brain is malleable. It's like a muscle—as your biceps hypertrophy after a gruelling workout, so does the mind after a mind workout. The volume of grey matter changes daily as branches of 86 billion neurons expand or contract, depending on the extent to which they are nurtured through mental exercises.

If the benefits are real and perceptible, then don't you think we should dedicate more time and effort to develop our mind rather than getting obsessed with our body? Of course, we should.

The stark reality is that this tiny organ at the top controls the entire structure beneath it. In fact, even your muscle building hinges on brain building to a measurable extent—a fascinating fact most people are unaware of. No matter how many times a day you're hitting the gym or how many repetitions you're performing, you won't see much improvement in your muscle mass until your brain is actively involved in the exercise. The more you fire your neurons during exercise, the more intense is the spark to the exercising muscle, eventually scaling up its capacity to lift massive weights, helping in faster muscle building. Plus, when your mind is in sync, you can continue your workout for a longer time with more focus and concentration without getting distracted by negative thoughts.

The following anecdote highlights the danger of not being committed to mind development.

The story is about an immensely talented weightlifter.

He started preparing rigorously for the Olympics well in advance (two years before the start of the event), and put himself into a highly competitive environment. He was a world champion in his weight category and was confident and desperate to win the Olympic medal for his country. A genuine prospect. A safe bet for the media pundits and fans. All the people who had heard his name or seen him—his social media fan club, people from his native village, childhood friends, colleagues, journalists, and even the President of the country he belonged to—were highly optimistic about him, predicting his victory and invincibility. He was riding high on the wishes and expectations of millions behind him.

However, on the day of the competition he failed to qualify for the finals. Retrospective analysis proved that his personal coach neglected key aspects of mind training while coaching him. Although he was a world champion in his weight category, he had failed to tame his self-doubt and negativity during high-pressure moments in the Olympic finals. Because of this systemic neglect of mind training, he could not generate the necessary neural drive to activate his muscles to lift the desired weight. In a bid to achieve 100%, he did his 99% but discarded that critical 1% that is necessary for success.

Such is the significance of mind training. It is immaterial how prodigious you are in your domain or the degree of perfection, glory and eminence you have attained so far. What matters is that you cannot afford to ignore brain exercises in your fitness regime like this world champion did. And if you do that, you will lose like him when you compete in your own finals. That's why it is so necessary to make mindfulness a part of your physical training schedule. It delivers a spectacular advantage by keeping you calm and focused during the deciding moments of your ambitious goals.

Takeaways

- Fitness is the ultra-premium fuel that makes you hyper-charged throughout the day to execute goal-directed efforts.

- Make your own customized fitness week schedule that incorporates all essential elements like running, HIIT, mindfulness and yoga.

- Adding mind exercises like yoga and mindfulness brings staggering dividends in terms of improved focus and concentration and by switching off DMN—the part of your brain responsible for monkey mind.

PENCIL WORK

▪ Draft your weekly fitness schedule, in tune with the physical activities/sports that you're good at, and that you can sustain for a long time.

DIET: THE SECOND RECHARGE

A healthy and nutritious diet imbued with vitamins, minerals and antioxidants, not only prevents deadly illnesses like diabetes, hypertension and cancer, but also yields cosmic energy. It adds infectious radiance to your face, and you can work tirelessly with passion for hours and hours. A healthy diet eradicates laziness, inertia, fatigue and impulsiveness—the major impediments that halt the completion of our routine assignments. It's no wonder then that by having quality food, we can be at peak productivity and can finish our multiple daily goals easily.

Diet is the second ultra-premium fuel that makes us super producers.

But the sad part is that most of us don't follow the correct diet. Despite volumes of dietary philosophies circulating on the internet and social media, the average person's food spectrum and behaviour is quite unhealthy. While science and philosophy have evolved considerably, sociology has remained stagnant, making impactful change on ground nearly invisible. Everyone preaches different magical diets and vehemently endorses their benefits, but very few are actually practicing what they're preaching. We advocate salads to others but then become hypocrites and stand in long queues at Domino's, McDonald's and other fast-food restaurants. This unhealthy trend of eating refined, processed and fried products not only negatively affects our longevity but also ruins our horsepower and work efficiency.

Then there are some people who consume unwarranted Paleo and Keto diets in a frantic bid to flaunt their lean and slender physique. This is not a sane approach. The Paleo diet, rich in meat, fish, eggs, fruits and vegetables, was meant for hunter-gatherers when there was no farming and hence no dairy products and grains available. But we're not accustomed to absorbing and processing this diet anymore because of modifications in our genes over the past 10,000 years. Similarly, the Keto diet is for those who are obese and aiming for rapid weight loss, which is a debatable strategy because of the lack of sustained efficacy and lots of side effects like weakness, headaches, kidney stones and weak bones.

If Paleo and Keto are not ratified diets, what do we need to eat to become a super producer?

To leapfrog your productivity and energy, I would recommend you adopt the WHO-designed "balanced diet." My endorsement is based on the stupendous powers disguised in its components. Every particle of this diet has the phenomenal potential to transform you on physical, psychological and spiritual levels. A balanced diet is the best diet!

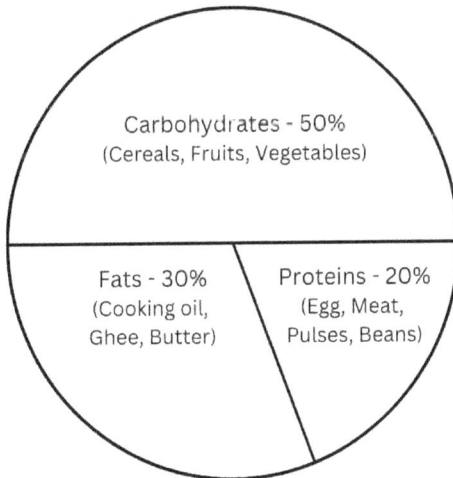

Carbohydrates - 50%
(Cereals, Fruits, Vegetables)

Fats - 30%
(Cooking oil,
Ghee, Butter)

Proteins - 20%
(Egg, Meat,
Pulses, Beans)

WHO RECOMMENDED BALANCED DIET

TAKE THE MIDDLE PATH

More is not always merrier. You must live a balanced life. And Buddhist philosophy has taught us that the right way to live that life is to take the middle path. This principle also applies to nutrition. Consuming a balanced diet, as depicted in the chart given in the previous page, is a judicious approach to living a healthy and productive life. You should not be living at the extremes of the dietary spectrum—for instance, consuming excessive amounts of protein, or indulging in a high-carb, high-sugar diet.

A high-carb diet is bad for health because it leads to obesity, diabetes and hypertension. A high-protein diet (with low carbs and low fats) also has pernicious long term effects. If we don't consume enough carbohydrates and fats, the brain stops working as it principally uses glucose and ketones (the products derived from the breakdown of carbohydrates and fats, respectively) as fuel. One morsel of useful information in this regard: our brain constitutes 2% of our body weight but burns almost 20% of the total energy even when we're resting. And if the brain is that of a genius, it may require more fuel because it is always hyperactive and operates in a thoughtful mode.

I have an interesting incident to share, enough to substantiate the relevance of carbohydrates for our brain. During the 1984 World Chess Championship in Moscow, the then-champion Anatoly Karpov and Garry Kasparov, two chess legends, competed for the crown and eminence. However, the championship was surprisingly called off abruptly, a disappointment for all the chess fans who watched it keenly, glued to their television sets.

Any idea why it would have been called off? The championship had to be aborted because Kasparov lost almost 22 pounds due to his over-stimulated brain that devoured calories like a voracious predator. Research has validated that elite chess players can burn more than 6,000 calories sitting down, as their brain is constantly exercising and orchestrating the next move to be executed against their opponent.

The bottom line is that carbohydrates are highly essential for your brain. And complementing the role of carbohydrates are fats, which provide the cushion of the myelin sheath to your brain cells. The sheath facilitates faster transmission of signals across neurons, eventually leading to better information processing and working memory required for multitasking. Carbohydrates and fats are both indispensable components for our composite growth and development.

This is the opportune time for you to shun Keto and Paleo diets—the fancy names with no scientific imprimatur or proven efficacy, broadcasted and propagated by social media pseudo-nutritionists. Instead, you must embrace this exquisite basket of the WHO recommended balanced diet as it is replete with the optimum amount of all essential nutrients and is relatively simple to follow and track as well.

As I wrap up this section, one last dietary hack that you can follow to recharge and rejuvenate yourself, before you put your first step of the day into your professional orbit.

FAST BREAK WITH BREAKFAST

What you eat for breakfast determines how fiercely you can fast break. Fast break is a very popular term used commonly in the game of basketball. It is a kind of offensive strategy where a player steals the ball and passes it to the fastest member of the team who then sets up fast break. Using sheer pace and dribbling skills, the player moves the ball into the opponent's court and scores a basket before the defenders can catch up.

Likewise, if you want to outpace all competitors in your domain and take a massive lead over them, you must unleash this offensive strategy of fast break and execute your plans and assignments at a blistering pace. A special breakfast that ignites your hunger and passion throughout the day will allow you to fast break into the league of pathfinders. Consumption of natural, fibre-rich carbohydrates like oats and fruits during breakfast releases glucose steadily in your blood stream, enabling you to work meticulously for prolonged periods without becoming mentally jaded.

In contrast to this, eating refined products like bread and sugar leads to a sudden glucose spike, that stimulates high bursts of energy during the first few hours of work. But very soon, when glucose levels drop drastically, it manifests in the form of lethargy, irritability and anger, which hampers productivity in a significant manner.

Your breakfast composition also determines one more thing: your league membership. Wondering how?

Well, across the globe, at every workplace, in every industry that produces goods or services that make GDP count, employees work in two different leagues. The first category is the Copper league. They show tremendous zeal at the start of the day, but the spark and radiance on their faces diminishes as sunset approaches, like copper gradually loses its lustre when exposed to moisture and air. By late afternoon, they look annoyed, and their threshold for expressing anger is very low, particularly when a situation demands a calm approach for problem-solving. They might be talented in their domain, and their integrity might be impeccable, but their productivity remains below par, and they become the Achilles' heel of the organization.

The second category is the Gold league. Members of this league are cheerful and highly kinetic, oozing pharaonic energy from morning to evening, which is as contagious to others as it is revitalizing to themselves. And despite working ceaselessly for endless hours, their facial glow never fades, just like 24-carat gold is never robbed of its perennial shimmer. Irrespective of the enormity of the problems and challenges they encounter, they function with extreme patience and aplomb. And they are definitely more productive and efficient than the Copper league members.

The composition of breakfast dictates your membership in either of the two clubs. A healthy breakfast that is saturated with berries, fruits, nuts and seeds and whole grain cereals is a license for entry into the Gold league. Otherwise, you become default members of the Copper league.

Takeaways

- Diet is the second ultra-premium fuel that delivers round-the-clock energy and enthusiasm required for goal-targeted endeavours.

- The WHO recommended balanced diet is the best diet.

- Remember that breakfast and fast break are closely interlinked. What you eat for breakfast determines whether you'll fast break ahead of your competitors in terms of productivity and efficacy.

PENCIL WORK

■· Take out a plain white paper and make a prototype of your food plate.

■· Begin by drawing a circle and divide it into two halves. Put carbohydrates in one half. Divide the second half into two equal portions for proteins and fats respectively.

■· Now carefully list your ingredients in each compartment like this:

Carbohydrates: cereals, vegetables, fruits

Fats: Olive oil, Ghee, butter, cheese, nuts

Proteins: pulses, beans, eggs, meat

■· Stick to this food plate every time you have a meal.

SLEEP: THE THIRD RECHARGE

Sleep is the third element to recharge your Graphene Mentality. To understand its enormous recharging potential, I would like to draw your attention to the sleep emoji.

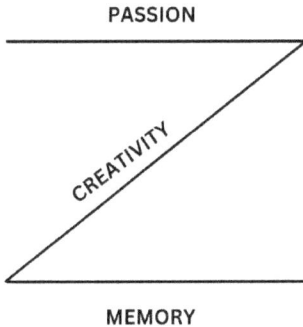

PASSION

CREATIVITY

MEMORY

- Passion (due to more energy after waking up from sleep)

- Creativity (due to peak imaginative power and flow state of mind)

- Memory (due to theta activity in memory storage site)

POWER OF SLEEP EMOJI $z^{z}Z$

This sleep emoji, which is so familiar to us courtesy of WhatsApp, is not just a symbol indicating sound sleep. It is suffused with colossal reserves of PCM: passion, creativity and memory.

Passion

Renowned sleep specialist, Dr Michael Breus recommends that an average person should complete at least 7.5 hours of sleep a night. When you sleep for this much time, you feel fresh and more energetic in the morning. You have abundant fire in your belly to fuel the passion required to perform goal-related activities throughout the day. Conversely, if you sleep less than the duration Dr Breus advises, you feel groggy and lazy all day.

Creativity

Optimum sleep allows you to enter the deep pocket of creative thinking, the ideal atmosphere to attain your peak imagination. To create a masterpiece, you need to master peace. To craft the magnum opus, you need magnum focus. History is witness to the fact that all noble ideas and revolutionary inventions have been products of the sleeping mind. It is in their sleep that writers have thought of the best stories worth writing, music composers have produced their greatest music, and mathematicians have discovered their novel theorems.

Why is the sleeping mind so productive?

The answer is obvious: it is free of ego, negativity, distractions, multitasking and noises of the external world that plague our conscious mind. It is calmer and more innovative. While we are sleeping, a sacred connection is made between our extrinsic goal and intrinsic soul. And when this intimate connection is established, our soul starts searching for all the ideas related to our treasured goal. It begins to invent solutions for the bottlenecks in our path to the esteemed destination.

Memory

The formation of goal memory is an intriguing process. It all starts with visualization in the amygdala. How do we wish to see ourselves in the future? What do we imagine and fancy in regard to our goals? Everything gets piled up in the amygdala during the day. When we sleep, these thoughts and images are sent to the hippocampus for processing and storage, resulting in the development of long-term goal memory.

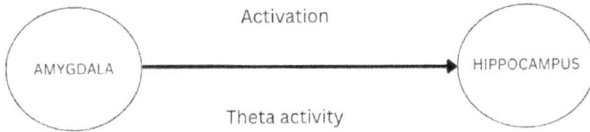

Emotional centre of brain
- It visualizes image/thought related to goal

Memory storage site
- Image/thought is consolidated into long term memory during REM sleep
- Goals get deeply embedded into our psyche

And when we drift away from our set goals because of the erratic nature of our mind, this goal memory helps remind us of our objectives. Through this process of active recall, we revert to our original trajectory and realign our priorities in the direction of our set goals.

Besides these triple wonders, there is one more clandestine benefit of sleep that you can channel to recharge yourself. That is Lucid Dreaming.

BECOMING A LUCID DREAMER

The science of night dreaming has never been amply elucidated in a better manner than by the famed psychoanalyst, Sigmund Freud. He propounded that "Dreams spring from wish fulfillment: we dream about what we dream of—a proposition that marries the two meanings of dream, the nocturnal wanderings of the unconscious mind and the motivated marches of conscious will."

He explained that our consciousness constitutes just the tip of the iceberg, and beneath this superficial and visible tip lies the vast pool of the unconscious and subconscious mind, with enormous power to produce magical stuff. During dreams, all our deep desires are manifested and we get an opportunity to travel to a different realm, which allows us to experience a tryst with our ultimate destination.

A different and more potent version of ordinary dreaming is lucid dreaming. It is a unique kind of night dreaming in which a person is aware of their dream and is conscious enough to modify or control its content, precisely the opposite to a normal dream where a person is unaware of the process. It is a form of meta-cognition.

Studies reveal that almost 55% of people experience lucid dreaming in their lifetime at least once. Scientists did not believe in this seemingly ludicrous concept until Dr Stephen LaBerge demonstrated it through his pioneering research in the 1980s. Since then, it has been employed in managing nightmares due to anxiety, stress, depression and PTSD (post-traumatic stress disorder). Psychotherapists use it to teach patients various techniques to remain awake during dreadful dreams so that they can mold the harrowing content of their dreams and make it more pleasant.

But more than its use in psychotherapy, lucid dreaming has been exploited by various luminaries to achieve their most hallowed goals.

Eminent artists like painters and musicians have effectively harnessed it to access the infinite potential of their subconscious mind and have produced masterpieces for humanity. In the same vein, extraordinary athletes create a mental arena in their dreams where they rehearse their entire training, envision delivering an outstanding performance, and fantasize the podium finish with the national anthem playing in the background. This helps to reinforce their neural pathways and re-wires their brain, making them obsessive about winning medals and inspiring them to execute when they step into the actual arena on the final day.

History corroborates that no one has mastered lucid dreaming more perfectly than the inventors did in the past. If you get an opportunity to travel to the US, you must pay a visit to The Edison & Ford Estates, a shared spot between best friends Henry Ford and Edison, in Fort Myers, Florida. Here, you'll find a banyan tree with a statue of Edison holding a stainless steel ball in his left hand. The anecdote behind the steel ball serves as a testament to the abounding power of lucid dreaming.

What Edison used to do with steel balls is very fascinating. Before sleeping, he would sit in his chair and hold a steel ball in his left hand, with a metal bucket placed underneath. As he brainstormed his intended invention, he would slowly drift into a transition state between wakefulness and sleep. Once his hands relaxed, the steel ball would drop into the bucket, making a sound that would disrupt his sleep. He would then quickly jot down any thoughts or ideas that had cropped up during the dream on a piece of paper that he always kept with him.

In his autobiography, *My Inventions*, Nikola Tesla, the prodigious scientist, confessed that he conducted various dream experiments where he visualized his inventions until he was sure they could be replicated in the laboratory. Similarly, Einstein's theory of relativity was also a result of his lucid dreaming. It enabled him to tap into the limitless ingenuity of his subconscious mind and discover this trailblazing theory that revolutionized our understanding of gravity forever.

AK Ramanujan, the mathematical genius, proved more than 3,000 theorems in his lifetime. But very few people know that the trigger for his genius was his habit of lucid dreaming. Throughout his life, he repeatedly dreamt of a Hindu goddess known as Goddess Namagiri Thayar of Namakkal, who presented him with complex mathematical formulas, which he could then test and verify upon waking. He admitted that the infinite series for Pi was also an outcome of this dreaming process. Describing one of his many insightful dreams, Ramanujan said, "...while asleep, I had an unusual experience. There was a red screen formed by flowing blood, as it were. I was observing it. Suddenly, a hand began to write on the screen. I became all attention. That hand wrote a number of elliptic integrals. They stuck to my mind. As soon as I woke up, I committed them to writing..."

All these anecdotes substantiate the latent power of lucid dreaming. You can also leverage this power to achieve your respective goals.

Dream about cracking any exam, IIT/JEE, CAT or NEET, and you will automatically generate phenomenal will to practice the thousands of mock tests necessary for cracking the exam. Visualize yourself as an astronaut and the day is not far when you'll be boarding a space flight and conducting breakthrough experiments at a location 400km above where you're sitting right now. Fantasize about reaching the summit of Mount Everest and you will discover that you have massive drive to embark upon back-to-back mountaineering expeditions until you scale the Everest.

There is nothing in this world that you can't accomplish after dreaming. Edison, Einstein, Tesla and Ramanujan all achieved because they were big-time lucid dreamers. You can also do it.

Takeaways

- Sleep is the third element to recharge your Graphene Mentality.

- Harness its triple wonders of PCM (passion, creativity and memory) to rekindle goal-directed efforts.

- Rehearse lucid dreaming to tap into the power of your subconscious mind.

PENCIL WORK

- Pull out your dream journal (if you don't have one, create one today itself) and endorse ONLY ONE goal that is most precious to you.

- Every night, before sleeping, make an intention to yourself, "I will dream about this goal tonight, and rehearse everything that is necessary to accomplish this goal in my dream."

IV.

POWER AND PROTECT

In this section, you will learn how specific tactics can power your Graphene Mentality to achieve micro and macro goals. And also why protecting your mentality against a devastating crash is so crucial for you.

POWER

'Most powerful is he who has himself in his own power.'
– Seneca

CHAPTER 10

Powering the Graphene Mentality

W‌hat you will learn in this chapter

- What is power?
- What are the tactics to power the Graphene Mentality?
- How can we use these tactics to accomplish our micro as well as macro goals?

Before we begin this chapter, one legitimate question—what is power?

In common parlance, power is synonymous with authority and the privileges people enjoy by virtue of their title or rank. When we think of paragons of power, we usually visualise kings and queens, land barons, business moguls, military generals, politicians, bureaucrats, judges, saints and spiritual gurus. They are considered most powerful in our society.

But is this real power?

No, it is not.

To understand power, I recommend you read Jocelyn Davis' book, *The Greats on Leadership*, which highlights the roadmap (through a step-by-step process) to becoming an ultimate performer. The author says, "Power is simply the ability to accomplish work and is not associated with title, rank or authority."

In the context of the Graphene Mentality, power lies in accomplishing your goals, both micro (short-term) and macro (long-term). With that in mind, we shall now discuss certain tactics to build this power.

BUILDING POWER TO ACHIEVE YOUR MICRO GOALS

Your strength and acumen in executing day-to-day micro goals dictates how powerful you are. And as we just discussed, it has nothing to do with your rank, professional qualification, authority, wealth or social connections. People who appear more powerful may be less powerful, and people whom we think less powerful are, in reality, more powerful.

Let me substantiate this statement.

Consider Lutyens Bungalow Zone—a cradle of power and prestige in India. It is where various ministers, parliamentarians, ambassadors, bureaucrats, senior army officers and other dignitaries formulate policies and make decisions to govern us. How much will a packet of milk cost us? At what age can we send our children to school? What all can we say on the internet? Which countries can we travel to? What businesses are we permitted to do? Can we have same-sex partners?

They have the authority to make all such decisions. They work in the British-era elegant edifices and live in palatial bungalows. When outsiders visit this area, they are usually awestruck by the perks and privileges these people enjoy, in stark contrast to what an average citizen outside this zone possesses. After witnessing this, they naturally wonder, "Wow! This is power! How can I become one of them?"

I felt the same two years ago when I moved to my new official residence inside the premises of The President's Estate— a magnificent complex right on top of Raisina Hill. But once I started living here, I realized that though Lutyens Bungalow Zone is the nucleus of power, not everyone working here is powerful. And most important of all, a person's rank and authority does not relate to their *actual* power.

For instance, a bureaucrat working from 9am to 5pm in the secretariat might be the most competent in the field. Still, it is not necessary that the bureaucrat would be efficient in completing the micro goals listed for the day. The reasons for inefficiency could be varied. Either it could be an inadvertent disruption in the routine due to random visitors and impromptu conferences; or it could be that the bureaucrat is following the wrong methodology while working. We might appear powerful from the outside, but only we know how powerless we are after failing to complete our work on time.

At the same time, there are many employees in Lutyens Bungalow Zone such as domestic help, sanitation workers, plumbers, firefighters and gardeners. These people are lower in rank, authority and status, and yet more powerful in executing their micro goals. They do their work on time in an impeccable manner and without any perks or privileges. I find my domestic help, Nisha, to be a perfect embodiment of this. Every day, she comes to my house at a fixed time, completes her work quickly and efficiently with incredible sincerity, and returns home to look after her kids.

What motivates her to do her work efficiently every day?

Of course, she has an incentive to do all this. I pay her money. But what is worth learning here is the terrific tactic she follows to complete her goals seamlessly. What she does is quite simple. She makes a clear and firm intention to do one micro goal at a time and sets herself an internal deadline to finish that before she proceeds to the next one. We shall discuss in detail this technique of hers in a short while.

Before that, I would like to make a statement: if we apply the definition of power propounded by Jocelyn Davis and forget about privileges for a moment, then Nisha is the epitome of power instead of the bureaucrat who works in elite spaces and yet struggles to finish tasks on time. If you too hold a prominent rank in a high-profile job, but are battling to finish your goals on time, then you must imbibe her methodology in case you want to be truly powerful like her.

POWER OF POMODORO

Pomodoro is the tactic Nisha employs while working and that makes her so powerful. It is the most efficient way to work on our micro goals lined up for the day. The unfortunate part is that despite its efficacy, this technique has not gained mass popularity. Even most of the ace workaholics who work with supreme industriousness at bullet speed, fail to capitalize on its benefits.

Let us see how, despite having administrative acumen, we ruin our productivity by not following this magical principle of time management. The problem begins in the morning itself. We start our day by selecting different tasks listed in our personal journal and relying on our elephantine working memory (with all vanity) to strive to complete all of them simultaneously. In a single burst of energy, we do multiple things—planning, drafting documents, making calls and meeting clients and visitors. It indicates our lack of patience to finish them one by one. We have this obnoxious habit of creating a massive bunch of files and reading them thoroughly in a bid to consume extraneous information that is not related to the task at all. In the evening, we return to our homes without finishing all the assignments that we planned at the start of the day, and the to-do list in our journal keeps expanding, only to add to our burden for the next day.

The malady is that our day-to-day efforts are spurred by this hackneyed myth: "Hard work is the only key to success." Thus, we consciously neglect potent smart-work tactics. Pomodoro is one such intelligent tactic that can deliver the maximum output in the minimum possible time.

Let me dig a little bit into the history of this stupendous strategy of time management. The story goes back to the 1980s, when an Italian named Francesco Cirillo used a tomato-shaped timer as his personal tool for micro-managing his routine. Pomodoro is the Italian word for tomato and that's how this technique got its name. Since then, it has been a philosopher's stone for all great time managers.

In this technique, a person focuses intensely on a particular task for 25 minutes until the timer rings. Whatever distractions (random thoughts) pop up during the session are noted on paper to ensure that the session is finished without interruptions. Then, a 5-minute relaxation break is taken for tea/coffee/replying to calls and messages over the phone. After that begins the second session to complete another ear-marked task until the timer rings again after 25 minutes. Like this, there are four sessions before you take an extended break of 20 minutes to refresh yourself. Each 25-minute interval is called Pomodoro. This is the duration Cirillo used to complete one task at a time, based on his specific requirements and attention span that allowed him to stick to this duration.

You can modify the duration in consonance with the nature of your work and your attention span. Some people do 40- or 50-minute Pomodoro sessions and then take a break. The big deliverable of using this tactic is that it steers you to complete various micro goals daily.

But there is one pre-requisite before you kick start your Pomodoro sessions. You need to design your Victory Clock, which depicts goals to be completed over 24 hours.

VICTORY CLOCK FOR MULTIPLE GOALS

Multi-tasking in today's world is taking a significant toll on our physical and mental health. It is one of the leading causes of

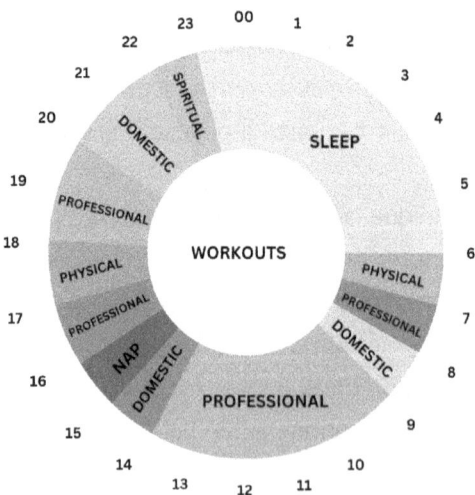

VICTORY CLOCK

the brewing epidemic of stress and depression. We are living in a time when our obligations and commitments are expanding faster than giant kelps (the underwater organisms that grow at a rapid rate of 60cm per day). With every passing moment, we are choking our already overwhelmed brains with additional goals. It becomes more onerous when these goals are heterogenous, spanning across various segments—professional, domestic, physical and spiritual. That last segment has become a necessity in the wake of this growing mental turbulence, manifesting through mass pilgrimages to Vipassana centers and meditation retreats.

Amid these challenges, Darwin's theory of survival of the fittest takes on a new dimension— it is no longer about physical strength but our adaptability in completing these goals of varied nature. Devising a personalized victory clock will guarantee your survival by making you proficient in tackling this massive workload and of course, enable you to live a peaceful and harmonious life. I'm sharing my victory clock below, which I use to complete my goals. You can use it as a template to make your own customized version.

Time	Workout	Activity	Goal achieved
0600-0700	Physical	Running, HIIT, Yoga, Meditation	Physical
0700-0800	Professional	Professional planning, brainstorming, listing to-do assignments for the day	Professional
0800-0900	Domestic	Breakfast and spend time with family	Domestic

Time	Workout	Activity	Goal achieved
0900-1400	Professional	Complete professional assignments	Professional
1400-1500	Domestic	Lunch with family Connect virtually if you are in a 9-5 job	Domestic
1500-1600		Afternoon Nap	
1600-1700	Professional	Resume professional assignments	Professional
1700-1800	Physical	Evening games	Physical
1800-2000	Professional	Complete pending tasks	Professional
2000-2200	Domestic	Dinner and spending time with family Household budgeting (clearing pending dues, planning savings and expenditures)	Domestic
2200-2300	Spiritual	Thanksgiving, gratitude, forgiveness	Spiritual
2300-0600		Sleep	

- Four key workouts—physical, professional, domestic, spiritual.
- Keep it flexible as well as firm (be firm with physical and spiritual workouts, but you can be flexible with professional and domestic workouts depending on workload).
- Keep Sunday for cleaning home, decluttering, visiting friends and relatives, watching movies or entertainment programmes.

Victory clock makes your 24 hours meaningful and worth living. Its itinerary has been designed in such an intelligent manner that activities that stimulate mind relaxation are scheduled before things that require brainstorming. Each workout feeds the successive workout, which feeds the next in sequence, and so on, creating a cascading effect that sustains your motivation to complete a variety of micro goals every day.

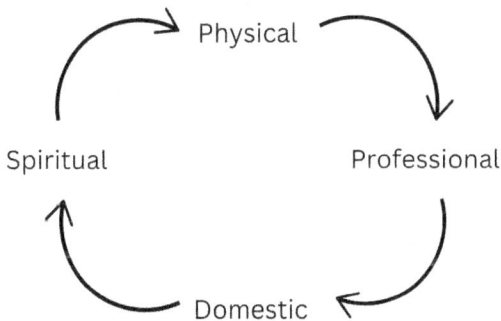

Physical

Spiritual   Professional

Domestic

The physical workout before a professional workout boosts serotonin levels and enables you to work free of stress and with greater productivity and efficiency. The domestic workout is scheduled immediately after the professional workout as an antidote against job-related mental fatigue. Playful interaction with kids, enlightening conversation with elders, and intimacy and lovemaking with your partner offer unique pleasure to offset the tedium that develops due to multi-tasking at the office. This leads to a quantum leap in your motivation levels, which you can leverage the next day to execute fierce sessions of professional workouts.

But why do we need the spiritual workout before sleeping?

Shouldn't be difficult to answer. It's a no brainer. Spiritual exercises help in forging a perfect harmony between our mind and soul, keep both in healthy shape, and assist in quick recovery from our overwhelming work schedule. When the mind is affected by the flood of workload, our soul is next in line and faces an imminent threat of drowning. They are intimately linked to each other like conjoined twins. When one cries in pain, the other also weeps. When we overburden our brain with too many commitments, we can hear this shrill cry from our soul, "Ok, it's enough! Stop it, I can't absorb it anymore." If we have an argument or fight with someone at our workplace and our mind is full of resentment against that person, then it is our soul that squeals, "Please get rid of this; I can't suffer it anymore." Spiritual workout through thanksgiving, gratitude, self-reflection and forgiveness keeps these twins happy and makes them work together for exponential output.

Every cycle of the victory clock adds a daily credit of a *sense of achievement* and *meaningfulness* to your personal account and builds hefty deposits in the long term for compounding gains.

So, design your own version of the victory clock (after factoring in your workload and the routine that allows it). And always keep a copy in your mind wherever you go. Block Pomodoro sessions for different kinds of workouts. Reserve one Pomodoro for the professional workout where you do only job-related assignments such as reading relevant literature, writing content, designing products, planning and formulating policies, or attending meetings. Keep another Pomodoro for the domestic workout where you fulfil domestic obligations like paying grocery bills, grooming your children, or spending precious time with your parents.

Just remember that during your sessions, you should do only that activity that you have intended to do. If you're doing a professional Pomodoro, you're advised not to pay your domestic bills or speak to your spouse until your session ends. Likewise, if you're thoroughly immersed in physical Pomodoro and sweating very hard, then do not spoil your session by attending to any incoming calls.

The rationale is that by allotting a fixed duration and creating mini deadlines for each micro goal, you generate a sense of urgency and build positive pressure to complete it. You defy Parkinson's Law that states that work expands to fill the time available for its completion. By setting Pomodoro, you purposefully reduce this time and create a competitive and challenging environment. And then your work automatically contracts.

By creating a firm intention and affirmation to finish one goal per Pomodoro, we tend to attain a *flow state*, a term coined by renowned psychologist Mihaly Csikszentmihalyi. In a flow state, there are no distractions and our concentration is supreme. And no matter how colossal the goal appears, it becomes less daunting in this state. A flow state enables us to sit for three hours in exams in a hyper-attentive mode and makes us experience timelessness, as if it was just three minutes. It is the flow state again which allows us to deliver a forty-minute presentation where we get utterly engrossed in our topic, unaware of what is happening outside that presentation room.

Attaining a flow state through Pomodoro delivers tremendous power to your Graphene Mentality and enables you to accomplish set goals and objectives in the minimum possible time. In this fast-paced, frantic world, the important thing is not just reaching your destination, it is also vital that you don't delay in reaching there. That you don't procrastinate! Because when you're moving towards your objective, you're not moving alone. An unlimited number of people are also moving in that direction, albeit at different paces, trying to out-compete each other.

To be the first to reach your target, you must unleash absolute devotion during each Pomodoro session. 25 minutes of intense involvement in anything, if done consistently, will make your achievements resonate for the next 25 years. But if you discard monomaniacal focus, sincerity, and the ferocity required during these 25 minutes, you might see your efforts fading into the air within the next 25 seconds.

Pomodoro is a powerful work strategy that allows us to achieve the daily micro goals scheduled in our victory clock.

But is there any powerful strategy to achieve our macro goals?

Of course there is.

BUILDING POWER TO ACHIEVE YOUR MACRO GOALS

Micro goals require intensity and focus, but macro goals demand patience, persistence and a ridiculous amount of discipline. And there is no better way of injecting power into your macro goals than following this excellent trilogy of will + drill + skill = kill.

will + drill + skill = kill

Every time I entered the training arena of 2 Para Special Forces (my previous regiment), I could not escape this captivating motto. It was not merely a catchy slogan. It was a viable formula that every soldier applied to build indomitable will, relentless drill, and flawless skill—the three essentials in getting a classical kill, a term used in the Indian Army for exterminating the enemy. The goal of the Special Forces warriors is to get as many kills as possible.

The entire arena was like a massive amphitheatre and various craftsmanship sessions would be running live in different corners. In one corner, a demolition expert explained about explosives used to pulverize brick and mortar structures and conducted mock drills to annihilate dummy hideouts. In another corner, soldiers would learn about the scientific principles behind different communication equipment, jotting down concepts related to the ionosphere and its role in the transmission of radio waves.

Similarly, there was a separate area for learning medical skills. Under the supervision of chief instructors, combat medics rehearsed life-saving procedures like CPR (cardio-pulmonary resuscitation), intravenous catheter insertion, and application of wound dressings.

These instructors were men in uniform who had already mastered their respective skills. And now they were on a tireless mission to disseminate the unique secrets of their crafts to fellow combatants, who were equally keen to assimilate nuanced concepts. In this manner, all relevant tactics of battle craft and field craft were transferred down to the lowest-rung soldier in the hierarchy. It would not be incorrect for me to draw an analogy between these instructors and Bodhisattvas, the enlightened monks who, instead of attaining Nirvana, took responsibility for teaching principles of enlightenment to their disciples.

Craftsmanship was the disciples actual religion, no matter whether they were Hindu, Muslim, Christian, Sikh or Parsi.

It could be gauged from the holy devotion they showed in attending classes conducted from Monday to Friday; Saturday was exclusively reserved for testing and evaluation of all skill parameters learnt during the week. This weekly testing process repeated throughout the year until all manuals and protocols related to their craft were consolidated in their long-term memory.

The whole exercise aimed to install salient skill tactics deep into their subconscious mind, to make them capable enough to retrieve and reproduce these tactics whenever the situation demanded. Craft competence was pivotal to them in terms of achieving speed, precision, cohesion and lethality—the key elements necessary to execute covert operations.

You can also use this spectacular formula of **will + skill + drill** to hone your craft and kill your macro goals in your respective domains.

Whether your goal is to become a flawless painter, or it is to become a remarkable coder, or you wish to become an immaculate surgeon, the only way to get to your destination is to apply this formula. Every day, demonstrate your will and practice your skill with complete drill and discipline, without inventing an excuse. If you do this, no one can stop you from becoming the best shooter in your segment.

WHY IS THIS TRILOGY SO POWERFUL?

When you apply this formula of will + skill + drill = kill, you're basically activating your mind loop in a subtle way, which allows you to persevere.

Mind Loop

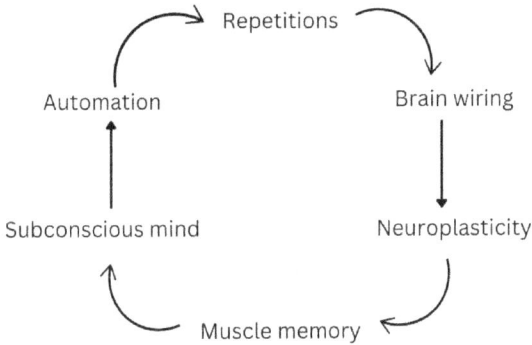

MIND LOOP

Repetition. Brain wiring. Neuroplasticity. Muscle memory. Power of the subconscious mind. Automation! This is the natural sequence of events that occurs before a person attains utter mastery in their craft. The daily repetition of the craft triggers the firing of neurons in a specific part of the brain. Neurons grow and expand in this region through a process called brain wiring or neuroplasticity, building huge reserves of muscle memory in our subconscious mind. And it is this power of our subconscious mind that helps in performing that skill in an automated mode and propels us towards our goal without hesitation and apprehension.

All legendary performers and fabled luminaries in history have followed this mind loop before achieving their most lofty goals. Without countless rehearsals through the mind loop, Thomas Edison could not have discovered the electric bulb, Nikola Tesla could not have designed the induction motor that powered the Second Industrial Revolution, Michael Phelps could not have won 28 Olympic medals, and Usain Bolt could not have run 100 metres in 9.58 secs. The trailblazing inventor James Dyson also relied on mind loop and developed 5,126 prototypes before he perfected cyclone technology in his 5127th attempt and created DC01—the world's first bagless vacuum cleaner.

I have only heard or read about Edison, Tesla, Phelps, Bolt and Dyson, and the persistence they exhibited while doing infinite mind loops. I have not seen them. But I know one close-knit community of soldiers who replicate mind loops day in and day out. After watching them closely for the last three years, I can say with confidence that practicing mind loops eventually begets enormous payoffs in the long run. Let's talk about this community, The President's Bodyguard—the oldest cavalry unit and senior-most regiment in service of The Honourable President of India.

Since 1950, every year, on the occasion of the Republic Day ceremony, almost 50-60 cavalrymen of this regiment, mounted on their majestic horses, assemble at the forecourt of The President's house. It's a treat to watch while they escort the head of the state to the saluting dais. They march with extreme synergy, exquisiteness and glory on *Kartavaya Path* (a magnificent road between North and South Block on Raisina Hill, right up to India Gate and the National War Memorial). Clad in their ceremonial uniform, they look simply elegant. A bright red long coat with gold girdles and white breeches, a blue and gold turban and Napoleon boots with spurs, along with a 10-foot cavalry lance in the right hand and a sheathed sabre on the left side of the saddle. If you're lucky to be there, you can see hordes of spectators capturing this unique moment while the contingent moves past, evoking awe and excitement in the crowd.

How come these cavalrymen succeed in putting up a spectacular show with laser-sharp accuracy? How do they control an animal ten times their weight and maneuver it to march in a single line with perfect synchronization and harmony? How do they achieve so much precision at an atomic scale?

Well, the secret ingredient of their immaculate performance is the willingness of both the rider and his horse to undergo thousands of mind loops, kicking off the first cycle when they are recruited and continuing it until they retire. The average recruiting age of a cavalryman is around 18, and that of a horse is around 4-5 years when he is inducted into the regiment from a high-quality breeding center. Every day, for 5-6 hours, the horses train painstakingly under the tutelage of experienced riders and learn all the necessary skills and minute procedures with the singular purpose—to display horsemanship of unparalleled quality. It is hard to believe that horses, through subtle cues of various kinds, can be trained to such an extent that they understand every command by their rider and respond in a desired manner. And it is difficult to imagine that sixty horses in unison can perform such complex maneuvers as walking, trotting, making a stop, and even saluting to the tune of the national anthem.

But when you have been powered by mind loops, everything is possible. PBG delivers a flamboyant performance every Republic Day because, 40-50 days before the day, they begin rehearsing the complete sequence of events, eliminating any scope for error either from men or horses. Through deliberate practice, they fire their neurons and build enormous muscle memory until they do it effortlessly.

"There is no regiment in this world which is as virtuous as PBG and which has so much commitment and will to fine-tune a given skill set," remarked the Commandant of the regiment, when I asked him categorically about the magical wand behind their flawless performance every time they march with their horses. "Our goal is not only to escort the President with absolute grandeur and regality on every big occasion, it is also to attain impeccable dexterity in our craft. We are the BEST in our business. And aim to do better than yesterday with every passing day. We don't just ride horses; we fly horses," he summed up as his face reflected pride.

Like PBG, if you also aim to reach the pinnacle of craftsmanship, there is no other way than to apply mind loops.

If your goal is to become a distinguished lawyer, you must keep advocating in support of your clients before you build enough expertise to put your arguments in a spontaneous mode. If your goal is to become a prodigious sales agent, pitch your product to potential clients every day because that is the only way to make them amenable to your power of persuasion.

If you want to become a top-notch chef, you need to spend at least 10,000 hours in the kitchen, as psychologist Anders Ericsson recommends, and do back-to-back cooking sessions until you develop your unique taste and flavour. And if you visualize becoming a successful guitarist like Jimmy Hendrix or Eric Clapton, you have to keep striking chords day and night until you achieve adroitness at their level.

Irrespective of your goal, keep travelling through the mind loop to discover a new version of yourself—one who is more loyal, romantic and committed to your craft, and who works in autopilot mode, driven by the power of the subconscious. The mind loop is the only viable method to tame the analytical conscious mind that generates excuses, rationalizations, doubts and fears, making you reluctant to perform repetitions.

One last and important thing regarding mind loops: like for every centripetal force, there is a centrifugal force; for matter, there is anti-matter; for protons, there are electrons; we have certain anti-loops for mind loops, too.

Anti-loop #1: Complacency

Complacency is the Achilles' heel of all champions. It is the feeling of self-satisfaction after the initial bout of success that makes champions less predatory and hungry when they step into the arena for the next bout.

On one night, champions are at the peak of a mountain, taking pride in their glorious accomplishments and hogging all the limelight. The following day, they wake up to find themselves lying at the rock bottom, feeling shattered after a steep fall from the peak of glory. It is not the gravitational pull or ferocious wind that causes their fall; it is the avalanche of complacency that dislodges them from the summit and throws them mercilessly into the nadir.

Andy Grove, Intel's former CEO, who revolutionized the semiconductor chip industry and drove Silicon Valley to magnificent fortunes, once said, "Success breeds complacency. Complacency breeds failure. Only the paranoid survives." The only thing that segregates phenomenally successful people from others is that they never cease to break their own accomplished goals. They never stop craving victory, even after remarkable triumphs in the past.

When it comes to killing complacency, I can't think of any other than great Michael Jordan. If you are a basketball fan, recollect epic game 5 of the 1997 NBA finals (Chicago Bulls vs Utah Jazz). Even if you are not fond of basketball, I would still recommend you browse YouTube and watch this iconic match. It offers a perfect glimpse into the tenacious mindset of this legendary player. Suffering from high-grade fever (103 degree F), he produced the rarest of rare performances of his life. Jordan had already won five NBA titles in the past. Yet his hunger to win the sixth one was palpable. And he did it in a heroic way, scoring 38 points. It is one of the most outstanding examples of persistence in the history of humankind that proves that legends are the epitomes of everything but complacency.

You should also perform like Jordan and not be complacent while chasing your lofty goals.

Anti-loop #2: Boredom

Persistence in practicing your craft and doing the same thing again and again brings boredom into your life. If that happens, you shouldn't abandon your craft forever. It's a flagrant betrayal. You shouldn't discard your goal when you cease to find excitement in your skill for, I believe that enduring the temporary pain of the mundane is the secret to reap the permanent joy of virtuosity.

Repetition brings listlessness, and no matter how exciting things appear to be at the outset, they fail to generate a dopamine surge after a certain period. It then creates a path for drudgery to settle, eventually erecting a divide between your ambition and your commitment. It is at this stage, when you feel jaded, that you must set a more challenging milestone to reignite your bored limbic system.

When you feel like you no longer have zest, you need to look up to and embrace this dictum—the path to stardom goes through boredom. Your persistence in pursuing your craft during prolonged spells of boredom will fetch your stardom. And make you a superstar! This is what heavyweight boxer Mohammad Ali felt and endured while perfecting every punch that bludgeoned opponents onto the floor in a ruthless manner. He confessed, "I hated every minute of training, but I said, 'Don't quit. Suffer now and live the rest of your life as a champion.'"

It was not at all exciting for him to follow his training regimen every day. It involved rising in the wee hours of the morning, running 5-6 miles down the street to the local gym, and then doing back-to-back sessions of shadow boxing, sparring, punching heavy bags, and skipping ropes, until he sweated profusely. He found it tedious to replicate all this day after day. But he could do it because he knew that the path to his stardom traversed through these lonely lanes of boredom. This training routine over 22 years made him the greatest boxer ever with 3 heavyweight championships, 56 career wins, and 36 knockdowns—a glorious feat that remains unmatched.

Takeaways

- Power is not synonymous with title, rank, authority and privileges. It is simply the ability to accomplish your micro and macro goals in a stipulated time frame.

- Use the Pomodoro technique to achieve your daily micro goals.

- Follow the trilogy of will + skill + drill = kill for your macro goals. It enables you to activate countless mind loops.

- While rehearsing mind loops, beware of two anti-loops: complacency and boredom.

PENCIL WORK

- Design your victory clock, highlighting the complete schedule of your four key workouts—physical, professional, domestic and spiritual. And follow this gorgeous routine for a meaningful life and immortal joy.

PROTECT

'To protect your energy... it's okay to cancel a commitment. It's ok to not answer a call. It's ok to change your mind. It's ok to want to be alone. It's ok to take a day off. It's ok to do nothing. It's ok to speak up. It's okay to let go.'

– Unknown

CHAPTER 11

Protecting the Graphene Mentality

W̶hat you will learn in this chapter

- Why protecting the Graphene Mentality is so important.
- What are the strategies that you can deploy to protect it.

When we relentlessly power our goal pursuits through the tactics of Pomodoro and mind loops, we tend to reach our breaking point. We all have a certain threshold and get exhausted after working in an unabated manner. In that situation, we need to step back and relax instead of continuously pressing the power button. We should go into a resting mode rather than staying in a fighting mode. We need to protect our atoms and let them sleep for a while before we think of reigniting them. Because our ability to showcase resilience, firmness and flexibility is finite, and if we exert ourselves beyond a particular limit, we will collapse.

In this regard, I would recommend three strategies that you can effectively apply to protect your mentality against a devastating crash.

1. TAKE A BREAK

Take tactical breaks when you feel burnt out after working incessantly for many weeks. Plan trips to serene and idyllic places in the mountains, islands or beaches, and discover spiritual bliss by spending some time in solitude. Fulfil crazy wishes in your bucket list. Do thrilling and adventurous activities such as skydiving, hiking, paragliding, surfing or scuba diving, to expand the limits of your fearlessness. Timely and intermittent breaks allow you to regain your lost vigour and enthusiasm and bring your motivation back on track.

In his book *The 4-Hour Workweek*, author Tim Ferriss coined a new term for these tactical breaks—mini-retirements. He proposed that instead of planning long-term retirement investments, one should focus on saving a small portion of one's accumulated wealth and take regular mini-retirements to fulfil wishes on the bucket list. After all, leisure is as important as work, recreation is as vital as a profession, and entertainment is as essential as infotainment.

Many iconic firms believe that taking frequent breaks is the magical formula for harnessing the maximum potential of their employees and extracting their peak productivity. CISCO has an innovative concept of a fun fund, which can be spent by employees on celebrations and fun activities. Intuit, a renowned tech firm, encourages all employees to spend 10% of their working hours pursuing an idea they are passionate about. Nike offers paid sabbaticals.

Not only firms, but all prolific leaders also schedule timely sabbaticals to take much-needed breaks from their hectic routines.

If you intend to be as productive as these iconic firms and prolific leaders, you must imitate this established trend of taking periodic breaks. These sabbaticals will allow you to fulfil your subconscious and hidden desires, which, if unfulfilled, will keep creating distractions in your ambitious goals. This is the cardinal reason why you need to complement vocation with vacation, and coalesce your working days with holidays, to make life more exciting and stimulating in the long term.

2. HEAL THROUGH FAMILY

While you conscientiously work towards your goals, apart from the usual burnout, you might also encounter certain catastrophic events: unexpected bankruptcy, shocking failures, or a severe illness. Usually, your family is the first line of defence against such calamitous events and absorbs the initial thrust and turbulence. Family includes your spouse, children, parents and grandparents, or it could be a pet if you are fond of keeping one. Although everybody plays a vital role, we shall discuss here the role of two key members in your family—your partner and your children.

Partner

When confronting any adversity, our partner's constant support plays a crucial role. We all know how their intimacy and warmth is the best ointment to heal our fractured heart and soul. But beside this, their support provides us strength and resilience during tragedy that protects us from a mental crash.

I know an Iron Lady whose life perfectly portrays how a partner should behave and respond during a crisis. Her name is Aarti Bal. Before we talk about her fortitude, let me first tell you briefly about her husband Col Navjot Singh Bal. He was my Commanding Officer and a valiant fighter. Unfortunately, he succumbed to osteosarcoma (a kind of lethal bone cancer) in March 2020. But he lived liked a spartan until his last breath. He is my real hero. A true paragon of The Graphene Mentality. While enduring an aggressive cancer, he executed iconic deeds worth disseminating through documentaries, for inspiration to those struggling with sagging spirits.

When his right arm was amputated and lungs were reduced to the size of peanuts due to the spread of the cancer, could you believe he ran a half-marathon with a smiling face?

Yes, he did it! And he did it in record time. Not only this, with his left hand, he practiced writing for countless hours in his office, honed his firing skills by shooting pistol bullets at dummy targets, and did all other routine chores like eating, bathing and driving, himself. Col Bal taught everyone who had seen him fighting this important lesson of how to find meaning to live and work in the moments when we're about to die. His life is actually an apt example of Victor Frankl's Logotherapy, wherein people try to discover their purpose to live even in the most miserable of circumstances.

He could do all this impossible stuff because he was lucky to have Aarti beside him. When his cancer was diagnosed and its news broke out, she handled everything in a calm and composed manner. No panic. No haplessness. No crying. No beseeching the Almighty for the magical intervention. She knew that the Titanic had met with an iceberg and it was sinking, yet she acted like a sturdy anchor to stabilize the turbulent ship. She groomed her kids and did not let tragedy affect them, provided unflinching care and support to the warrior husband, and often travelled with him across the length and breadth of the country for his treatment. As his condition deteriorated, she was an inseparable soulmate, rendering soft healing touches until he slept peacefully for eternity. His vital organs crashed, his heart ceased to pump, his lungs stopped breathing, his limbs could not move, but she was standing steady beside him. A big salute to the brave lady.

The crux of the story: your partner is the only person who will stay permanently with you until your death. Parents and grandparents depart, children leave home to pursue their career and settle separately, your pet will survive only 10-12 years. Your friends are transient and they will meet you once in a while. When no one is there to support you, you will have your partner. So, it is necessary that you make your partner an integral part of your healing process.

Children

During difficult times, the sight of our children's smiling faces can be very comforting. We feel a sudden relief—a breath of fresh air. In a flash, all the tension, resentment and grouchiness dissipate.

As a part of your domestic workout, you must spend some fruitful time with your kids. Take them for evening strolls. And don't be surprised if you get bombarded with such questions like, "Daddy, why is the sky blue?" "Why is it raining?" Or "Mummy, how is the rainbow formed?" "How do aeroplanes fly?"

Don't evade their questions. By engaging in intellectual interactions with our kids, we not only foster their inquisitiveness but also channel our minds away from negative thoughts. Scientific studies have validated that when parents encourage their children to explore or draw their attention to specific objects of their interest, there is a conspicuous surge in the oxytocin hormone. And oxytocin makes us happy. It heals everything.

A child is the real father or mother of a person. One thing that we can learn from our children is the art to live in the present moment. A child's sole motive is to discover joy in whatever little possessions they have: toys, teddies, marbles, cubes, candies, water colours, pencil or a pen, and create wonders out of these objects. And you will be surprised to see how, through their imagination, they incubate brilliant ideas, designs and drawings.

So why can't we take some time off from our busy schedule and simply do what they are doing in the moment? Why can't we stop time travelling in our minds and stay in the present? It's doable. Not laborious at all. And yet, we don't do it, ruining our peace and happiness. Most of the time, our anxieties and fears arise because we ceaselessly ruminate on the past and the future. We think too much about past failures and future expectations and then it all spirals out of control.

3. HIRE A COUNSELLOR

When you're going through a terrible phase, if you're hesitant to speak to your family members or friends, you can choose this alternative. If you are afraid of exposing your vulnerability and weakness to your intimate circle, then seeking the help of a good counsellor is an ideal option for you.

I have a very close friend who was in extreme mental turmoil after a rift in his personal life. He had recurrent bouts of anxiety and suicidal thoughts, which bothered me as much as it distressed him. I got an inkling about his depression when he suddenly stopped turning up for the evening football game, a routine he was passionate about. Anhedonia, or the loss of interest or pleasure in routine activities, is a common symptom of depression and is a signal to seek remedial action ASAP.

When I inquired about his problem, he confided that the differences and friction between him and his wife had ballooned out of proportion, and he felt as though he was trapped in a long, gloomy tunnel. He admitted that he had been crying ceaselessly for the last week and had hardly slept. I sincerely recommended that he seek the help of a psychological counsellor who, I thought, would be the best person to render appropriate therapy and cure him. After all, I missed his fierce competitiveness on the football field and wanted him desperately as a striker on my team.

Anyway, he was a bit apprehensive about my idea and was reluctant to talk about his ailment to the psychotherapist. Instead, he preferred the following escape strategies: he watched entertainment videos on YouTube, listened to soft and soothing music, did a few meditation sessions on the virtual platform Headspace, and occasionally drank alone. He did all this to evade the chaos and divert his attention away from the real issues. To flush out the internal commotion in his mind, he even resumed playing soccer for a while, with the hope that the toxins would be released through the sweat pores and he would feel better. But things don't work that way.

Eventually, all these escape strategies failed in eradicating his woes, and tension kept piling up, leading to frequent domestic bouts between him and his wife. And like other people who follow such escape strategies, he ended up accentuating his agony, as his suppressed thoughts kept haunting him. The fundamental problem was that he was not willing to articulate his thoughts to anyone and did not deem it necessary to do so.

After many rounds of persuasion, he acceded to my insistence and sought the help of a trained counsellor. He and his wife shared all the contours of their turbulent relationship with the doctor, and finally, they consented to undergo psychotherapy sessions and all other necessary healing protocols. After treatment, I could see a measurable improvement in his overall mood, facial expressions and lifestyle. He was hale and hearty, his relationship was no longer strained, and he was back on the football field as a striker, making awesome moves with his usual aggression.

Counselling helps a lot!

That's why it is an integral part of the protective shield. It provides a robust safety cover to your atoms of resilience and firmness. With its support, you can resume your journey even if you are stuck in dire straits. But the disheartening part is that people don't seek counsellors regarding their mental health, even though they book counselling sessions for education, career, nutrition, sports and de-addiction. We are hesitant to acknowledge and share our mental frame with others, including experts.

It's high time we start thinking about hiring a personal counsellor to whom we can vent our feelings and empty the emotional baggage inside our mind. It would be a significant capital investment with both immediate and long-term returns. Buying stocks or property can build your physical capital, but purchasing a comprehensive personnel counselling package will amplify your psychological capital by leaps and bounds.

Author Tim Tamashiro, in his book *How to Ikigai*, weighs the benefits of a counselling membership over a gym membership, and laments the trend of millions signing up for a year's worth of treadmill torture at the local gym. And then only 18% of them use their membership regularly. He points out that the money people spend buying gym memberships could buy them an adequate number of counselling sessions, and benefits from these sessions would persist for years. When you leave each session, you get a little life coach that stands on your shoulder and reminds you of the stuff that makes you happy. The author puts this interesting question: "What if, at the beginning of January each year, hundreds of psychologists offer deep discounts for annual counselling membership packages for your well-being?"

Imagine the amount of learning and personal growth it would bring to your life.

Takeaways

- When you power your goal pursuits in an unfettered way, there is a high likelihood of mental exhaustion.

- There is a limit to which you can fire your atoms of firmness, flexibility and resilience. They need to be protected against a complete shutdown.

- In this regard, there are three protective strategies— take a break, heal through family and hire a counsellor.

PENCIL WORK

- Like you marked stress weeks in your calendar, designate two weeks every six months when you will take complete breaks from the hustle and grind and go on sabbaticals to serene mountains and islands, or do adventure-filled, high-adrenaline stuff.

- Choose four-five substantially selfless people (your family members, friends or mentors) who you can trust and share your sorrows, despair and grief with, without thinking twice. List their names, engrave them deeply in your mind, and develop these relationships with extreme tenderness and care. They are the ones who form your protective shield.

CHAPTER 12

Conclusion

Now that we have decoded the core attributes of the Graphene Mentality (firmness, flexibility, resilience and team spirit) and its supporting elements (ignition, recharge, power and protection), we have come to the end of our detailed analysis of this trailblazing mindset. Here is a perfect and ideal template that is so necessary to accomplish your goals, be it micro or macro, professional or domestic, physical or spiritual.

I never thought that things could be so simple and streamlined to execute; but they are, if we internalize the values, rituals and tactics which this mentality encapsulates. I never expected that goals, no matter how colossal they appear, could be easily achievable if we embrace the structured and methodical approach this revolutionary mindset entails. I never believed that values like flexibility and resilience, along with rituals like GPS and LGF, would ever be so potent in rekindling my spirit after crushing adversities. I never realized that constant ignition and daily recharge of our mindset is so necessary to re-energize our goal-targeted efforts.

Most importantly, I never imagined that with the mammoth power of the Graphene Mentality, I would ever be able to achieve my ultimate goal of becoming a writer. So, I will conclude this book by sharing how I leveraged this mentality to overcome all the challenges I encountered while writing it.

Well, I am passionate about writing. It's a sublime art that allows me to grow and expand my creativity. It also provides me the opportunity to connect to my soul and express myself, whether I am happy or sad. And at the end of the day, writing delivers immense satisfaction after I have penned down words and ideas worth spreading. But before the start of this project, I had written only a few pages or articles for various magazines. I never contemplated writing a complete book on a singular subject.

Let me honestly admit that writing about 50k words was indeed a Herculean task. My experience during this journey bears eerie similarities to what I went through while doing the 40km endurance run during the paratrooper's probation in 2011. For me, writing a book was more like a marathon and not a 100-meter sprint. It was a test of my patience, resolve and mental tenacity more than of my speed and intensity. It was a test of my Graphene Mentality.

As the Graphene Mentality advocates doing preparatory homework of P2P before embarking on our goals, I concretely formulated my P2P. I knew that the delineation of purpose was extremely important if I had to write consistently and with passion. My P2P was simple. I wished to crystallize the scientific properties of the element graphene into cardinal values that are essential in accomplishing our goals and crafting a successful and happy life. And then amalgamate these values into a distinctive mindset.

Every day, I activated my atom of firmness to write something creative and meaningful related to my subject. However, I did not opt for a rigid posture and never tried to write 1000 words before going to bed, as some writers do. Plus, I was not finicky about a specific place and time of the day to translate my thoughts into paragraphs. I kept it flexible. I wrote at all these places: office, home, playground, parks, highways, trains, flights, airports, hotels, restaurants, hills and beaches. And I wrote whenever I felt comfortable, whether early morning, afternoon, evening, or late night. My frequency of writing varied from 200 words to maybe 700 words per day. There were some days in between when I found it difficult and cumbersome to write even a single sentence. And in the way that water droplets stop moving through blocked pipes, my words, too, failed to move smoothly through my clogged brain.

Worse, when I was about to finish my book, I felt like quitting my project. The reason was that I was out of fresh ideas and concepts, and I felt mentally exhausted after writing every day. My self-belief was shaken, my decision pillar trembled with the fear of failure, and I behaved like a pendulum, oscillating from one negative thought to another.

Complicating the situation further, MS Word on my MacBook, where I typed and saved the entire draft manuscript, crashed suddenly. Along with it crashed my hopes and aspirations of writing a book. I was rudderless and could not find any way to navigate the storm, except going berserk and shuttling with my MacBook from one Apple care center to another in complete panic. The Apple service staff, too, was helpless and could not retrieve the files. I felt extremely dejected and guilty, for it was my blunder to not save the draft onto iCloud. That was the most agonizing phase of my journey. The mission seemed impossible.

At this juncture, the atom of resilience extricated me from that awful phase. I resorted to the GPS ritual for a few weeks before I could muster the courage to write again. This ritual bailed my self-imprisoned mind out of the shackles of despondency and energized me to incubate new ideas. Apart from taking a tactical break of a few days and the constant psychological support from my family and close friends, it was the face of Maximus that injected life back into my ambition.

Maximus is my three-year-old Golden Retriever who has always been there for me. When I return from the office, he is the first to appear at the door with his signature pose—lying supine with all four legs raised, a reinforced behavior developed due to the belly massage he has been receiving since I brought him home from a local breeder. Maximus is the most potent element in my psychosocial support system. I feel incomplete and dead without him. It was his smile that triggered my zeal and intent to sit for back-to-back Pomodoro sessions and enabled me to rewrite the entire manuscript.

Lastly, it was not merely my aptitude and perseverance that made it possible. There were dozens of selfless people around me who were instrumental in reshaping and polishing the content. It was not my solitary effort. It was team work. Mrs Abha Ayenger, who did two rounds of word-by-word copyediting. Pheji, chief editor at Jaico, who believed in me enormously, gave me pragmatic tips for refining the narrative, and was patient enough to review my revised drafts over and over again, until I could make it compelling. Mrs Dhruti Zala, Mr Vishal, and Mr Abhinav, who helped with designing illustrative sketches and diagrams. My parents who encouraged me to write consistently and pushed me to get back on the track whenever I tended to be complacent. My wife, who was remarkably supportive throughout this journey and who took all the pain in this world to nurture and groom

Viraj single-handedly so that I could get the adequate time to write. And the organization where I'm currently working, which granted me ample freedom, time, and experience to compose and produce ad libitum. All credit goes to them. They are the domestiques of my Tour De France. It is not me; it is they who summoned all the resources in their armory to ensure that I reach the finish line triumphant and unharmed.

This was my experience. This is how I used the Graphene Mentality to fulfil my glorious dream of writing a book.

How do YOU intend to launch it in your life?

The Last Homework
A Tribute to the Pencil

Implementing the Graphene Mentality in your life is the final and most important homework. As I told you at the beginning of this book, learning concepts can only make you a theoretical Czar, but execution will make you a practical King. Do it, and that will be an ultimate tribute to the Pencil you own- the source of this epic mentality.

I can only guide you systematically, while the real work must be done by you.

The systematic approach involves following these four basic steps along with four supplements.

Four Steps

STEP 1- PLAN

Choose your goals through P2P exercise. Discover your passion for which you are willing to persevere every day, which can drive you forward even if you get bored while pursuing it. Find a constructive and meaningful purpose which can propel your passion 24x7x365. And then demarcate clear and concrete goals in perfect alignment with your passion.

Select variety of goals to live a fulfilling and enriching life. Goals could be micro: doing 50 pushups every day, reading 20 pages every morning, spending a quality hour with your family before sleeping, or devoting 10 minutes every day to housekeeping. Or they could be macro: reading ten books a year, running one half-marathon every six months, spending 3,000 hours every year honing professional skills, or going on a week-long family trip to some exquisite destination every summer.

In addition to individual goals, you must also incorporate some societal goals into your blueprint of success. This could be donating 1% of your annual income to charity, mentoring five school children and helping them build careers, or giving your surplus clothes and grains to homeless and hungry people.

You must do this because society needs you more than you need yourself or your family needs you. Be a team warrior and not just a solo performer, for absolute bliss lies not in swallowing your accolades but in the gratification that comes from the progress of others through your contribution. Personal goals will take care of your physical, domestic and cognitive workouts. Societal goals, when accomplished, will cater to your spiritual workout by instilling a sense of fulfillment, thus helping you execute all four critical workouts in your victory clock.

STEP 2- EMBARK

After doing preparatory planning through P2P, embark on your goals by activating your atom of FIRMNESS. Once you have begun, be firm like a pillar in persisting with your goals. Do not behave like a pendulum, oscillating from one goal to another, even though 4D monsters (delusions, deficiency, detractors and distractions) will try their best to push you in that trajectory.

STEP 3- ENDURE

Endure your rigorous goal journey with the atoms of FLEXIBILITY and RESILIENCE. Be mentally prepared to face massive stress and setbacks- an inevitable part of goal-chasing process. Practice dealing with stress through rehearsing Stress Weeks throughout the year. To navigate setbacks, resort to ritual of LGF (Live, Give and Forgive) and most importantly, activate your GPS.

G- Practice GRATITUDE by reminding yourself that you are not the only one who is affected by setbacks; rather, there is a separate, big continent of such people existing on this planet.

P- Seek help of core members in your PSYCHOSOCIAL support system, who not only console you but also inoculate you with the necessary courage to fight back.

S- Cultivate immense SELF-BELIEF by recollecting your legendary performances in the past and evoking your talents.

That's all you need to craft your resurgence and rekindle your instincts.

STEP 4- COOPERATE

Whether you are chasing a personal goal or striving to achieve a collective goal, cooperate through the atom of TEAM SPIRIT. Because, as I said earlier, companionship is more worthwhile than one-upmanship. Eleven mediocre people operating interdependently are mightier than one genius working independently. Winning is not an individual game, it's a team game. It is not a solitary battle; it is a collective war! You need to cooperate with your colleagues selflessly, for it is the most economical and efficient method of winning, and an effortless and speedy way to reach your destination.

Four Supplements

IGNITE – While you are doing your routine work in pursuit of your coveted goals, always use the power of communication to IGNITE your atoms. Assume robust body language, encourage yourself through powerful speeches, and have a peek at your quotes to elevate your spirits.

RECHARGE – Every day, RECHARGE yourself with fitness, diet and sleep—the three critical ingredients of fuel for your Graphene Mentality. Formulate a customized fitness regime and a healthy dietary plan to harness the energy and focus required for your goal-targeted endeavors. Sleep adequately to avail its triple benefits, passion, creativity and memory (PCM), and practice lucid dreaming to unleash its inherent wonders.

POWER – Learn to leverage the POWER of the Graphene Mentality to accomplish your micro and macro goals. Sit for plenty of Pomodoro sessions every day to complete your micro goals listed in your victory clock. And to crack your long-term macro goals, apply the fabulous trilogy of will + skill + drill = kill, powered by mind loops.

PROTECT – While you are ferociously powering through your goal pursuits, find the protective strategies that will keep you safe against any mental crash. When you are overburdened with stress, take a sabbatical, seek relief through your family, or hire a trusted personal mentor or counsellor. At regular intervals, adopt a resting mode and renounce your fighting mode, before you revitalize yourself to resume your sweating sessions.

If you are willing to do all this, the Graphene Mentality will propel you into the orbit of success and heroism. Go and trigger its atoms!